When this you see

remember me

GERTRUDE STEIN

in person

Gertrude Stein at Bilignin
singing "The Trail of the Lonesome Pine"
photograph by the author

BY W G ROGERS

When this you see

remember me

GERTRUDE STEIN

in person

GREENWOOD PRESS, PUBLISHERS
WESTPORT, CONNECTICUT

Grateful thanks are expressed to the following publishers for permission to reprint material from their publications:

To The Conference Press, Sherman Oaks, California: for permission to reprint an excerpt from "Identity A Poem" from WHAT ARE MASTERPIECES, copyright, 1940, by Gertrude Stein.

To Random House, Inc., New York, New York: for permission to reprint an excerpt from PORTRAITS AND PRAYERS by Gertrude Stein, copyright, 1934, by the Modern Library; and for permission to reprint an excerpt from "Tender Buttons" from SELECTED WRITINGS OF GERTRUDE STEIN, edited by Carl Van Vechten, copyright, 1946, by Random House, Inc.

To Charles Scribner's Sons, New York, New York: for permission to reprint an excerpt from A FAREWELL TO ARMS, by Ernest Hemingway, copyright, 1929, by Charles Scribner's Sons; and for permission to reprint an excerpt from PARIS, FRANCE by Gertrude Stein.

124 200

Originally published in 1948
by Rinehart & Company, Inc., New York and Toronto

Reprinted with the permission
of the author, William G. Rogers

First Greenwood Reprinting 1971

Library of Congress Catalogue Card Number 72-139145

SBN 8371-5761-7

Printed in the United States of America

This book about my friend Gertrude Stein would not have been written without the consent of another friend, Alice B. Toklas, and could not have been written without her help. Last spring in Paris Miss Toklas painstakingly went over the manuscript with me; charitably refrained from objecting to opinions of mine with which she disagreed; and severely charged me with devoting too much space to her. This is not about Miss Toklas, she argued, and Miss Toklas must be kept in her place. I am sure Miss Toklas has been kept in her place; to write about Miss Stein without Miss Toklas would be comparable to writing about Pollux without Castor.

My principal sources for this picture of the unforgettable Gertrude Stein are, besides her creative works, our personal relationship and her two hundred and more letters and postcards to me, which will be deposited with the Stein collection of the Yale University Library.

They are addressed to "Kiddy" or "Kiddie," as Miss Stein and Miss Toklas called me, behind my back, in 1917 when, I hardly need explain, the appellation was not so inept as it has since become. They were written in pen and ink, scratched off rapidly in a sprawling and nearly illegible hand. Miss Stein used any kind of paper, thin or thick, blue or white, typewriter size or smaller, ruled or plain; sometimes it was headed with the "rose is a rose" device set in a circle, or a rubber-stamp "Bilignin par Belley," or the Paris address, 27 rue de Fleurus.

The curious variety of pictures on the postcards testifies to Miss Stein's heterogeneous taste. There are photos of portraits of Miss Stein and paintings by Corot, Ingres, Zurbaran and Goya; a Chartres statue; a 12th-century church interior; Chambéry and Vaucluse architecture; views of French towns; the home of Miss Stein's brother Michael; a "Palais Ideal," a toy castle; puppies; some staves of Massenet; "Unser Volkskanzler Adolf Hitler" standing in civvies on the shore of an Alpine lake; some youngsters playing war, entitled "La Bataille de la Marne."

Miss Stein often spelled in an unorthodox way, cut "excited" to "xcited," ignored English forms of capitalization, and sometimes left her sentences incomplete, though they were always as plain as day. I have followed her epistolary styles exactly. My explanatory remarks are in brackets. Chapter headings and title are direct quotations from Stein works, conversation or letters.

The assistance of my wife, Mildred Weston, has been so invaluable that she becomes, in effect, co-author. Her acquaintance with Miss Stein was shorter than mine, but in some respects more apperceptive, and she has amplified and sometimes modified my interpretations.

Miss Stein's letters contain the permission to make use of them.

New York
December, 1947

Contents

When this you see

remember me

GERTRUDE STEIN

in person

$\mathcal{W}$E WOULD LIKE YOU TO HAVE TEA WITH US

1

THE ODD combination of a flat tire and what is perhaps an inordinate interest in Latin was responsible for the two crucial, directive moments in my thirty-year acquaintance and friendship with Gertrude Stein and Alice B. Toklas.

Chronologically the puncture came second. The nail was lost by a farmer's workhorse clopping along a hot, dusty road in southeastern France; the nail was picked up by the wheel of a Ford driven by a squarish, monumental woman; the train to Paris was missed; and the long, earnest talk which otherwise would not have taken place was held in the thin shade of a tree in a station yard.

The business about the Latin begins in some vague past indeterminate now beyond the fact that classes started for me in high school, where languages were entertaining, or at least not difficult, and science and mathematics were dull. The Latin led to French, the two marched along together in college, and no doubt helped importantly at the end of my junior year to induce me to abandon campus for camp and volunteer for service in the first World War.

The consequence was that by the fall of 1917 I had seen St. Nazaire, Chartres, Versailles, a bit of Paris, and a lot of Châlons-sur-Marne and the front just beyond it and, having been on French soil for six months, was entitled to a furlough. Granted under the combined rules of both the French and American military, it added the lets of one to the hindrances of the other, but still had some advantages. My outfit, an ambulance unit attached to the French army, was stationed in the Champagne sector, geographically, and happily in the champagne sector, too. Like everyone else I would have preferred to visit Paris with its artistic and historical monuments and fleshpots, but unappreciative or selfish brass placed the near-by capital out of bounds.

There were several reasons for choosing Nîmes, though I could not have guessed the one which mattered most. It was about as far as a man could run from the mud, work and noise of the front without leaving the country. It was so far, at any rate, that travel time, which the considerate French allowed in addition to the basic two weeks, would increase generously the over-all duration of the holiday. Since the trip called for a change of trains in Paris, the alert soldier, however inexperienced, by pretending to misread timetables could spend one night there going and another coming without the risk of a third night in the jug.

Furthermore, it offered some of the most imposing

4

and least ruined Roman ruins. Here was my Baedeker: Nîmes, surrendered in 121 B.C. by the Gauls to the Romans, has an arena, or "arenas" as the French misleadingly express it, variously attributed to Antoninus, Trajan, Vespasian, Titus and Domitian; the incomparable Maison Carrée, the Midi's priceless architectural gem; luxurious baths, and extensive gardens rising to the lofty Tour Magne from the summit of which, if your legs can climb it, you can see, if the weather is clear, the faint blue line of the Mediterranean off to the south. Within fifteen or twenty-five miles are the three-tiered, majestic Pont-du-Gard, one of Rome's grandest bequests; the city of Arles with arena and theatre, and Aliscamps' crumbling grave stones with Latin inscriptions; and Orange with its magnificent theatre—"the most beautiful wall in my kingdom," Louis XIV declared with unabashed pride and undeniable accuracy.

I never found out whether it had fleshpots, but that was not the fault of Gertrude Stein. Just twenty years later on our "sentimental journey" with her, she and Mildred Weston remained absorbed in a conversation to which I gave only the better half of my attention while we traipsed through Avignon's red-light district at the hour when painted dolls and molls, undressed for business, lolled in lighted doorways.

But it did have Miss Stein, in person, and I might add to the usual list of the benefits of a classical education the surprising fact that mine introduced me to Miss Stein. On the other hand, it did little or nothing to prepare me for a woman of her extraordinary character. Whether it helped me to understand her writing is another matter; I would not say no, I would say not much. Yet there must be harder ways of arriving at "rose is a rose is a rose" than through *bonus, bona, bonum.*

That encounter was of such importance to me that even now I am not sure whether I can estimate correctly its full extent. I can be sure of only one thing: it resulted in some of the richest experiences of my life, and one of my warmest friendships.

2

The all-night ride in a third-class compartment, with a window knocked out and bare wood benches too crowded for lying down and too hard for sleeping or even snoozing while sitting up, took the gimp out of this soldier boy by the time he reached Nîmes. Here was all he had longed to see, and it was dawn, but the wonderful sights barely registered as he dragged his weary feet along the local railroad street to the Hôtel du Luxembourg, the city's finest, where he engaged a room, the hotel's cheapest, and tumbled into bed.

Early in the evening he followed a pair of oddly dressed women from lobby into dining room and thus for the first time laid surprised and amused eyes on Miss Stein and Miss Toklas.

Though both were short, one had twice the girth of the other. The sturdy and stocky Miss Stein walked with a slow, deliberate tread, as if walking were more than a means of locomotion. Miss Toklas, slight, wiry and nervous, moved with a quicker step. Viewed from the rear, it was tramp tramp tramp against a canter, ponderous half notes overlaid with lively eighths. After nodding cordially to a French general, who sprang up from his chair by the opposite wall and saluted, they reached their corner and sat down.

American private first class, quite as conspicuous for my rumpled and wrinkled bag of a khaki uniform as the two women were for their costumes, I touched hand to forehead in formal greeting to everyone—"Messieurs, 'dames"—after the fashion of my French comrades-in-arms. A waiter guided me to a lonely table, where I ordered and ate a hearty dinner and throughout buried my nose in a yellow, paper-covered book.

Since it was wartime, the hotel had few patrons, but Miss Stein and Miss Toklas marched and skipped daily to their places. Accustomed to a tarnished mess kit, dingy regulation knife, fork and spoon, the side of a box for table and at best my lap for my tablecloth, I enjoyed immensely the luxury of white linen, clean china, gleaming silver and uniformed waiters, yet I was increasingly mindful of the two women and stole at them inquisitive, stealthy glances which it may be they likewise stole at me. So this is France, I said to myself, and reflected confidently on the broadening effects of travel.

On my second day I left for the Pont-du-Gard and the town of Uzès; on my return on the fourth day, the women introduced themselves.

"I am Miss Toklas," the smaller one announced formally, "and this is Miss Stein."

I bowed, and we shook hands.

"You are the first American soldier we have seen in Nîmes," she continued, "if you are an American soldier."

They were right, I agreed, I was an American soldier, and I told them my name and what I was doing at the front and in Nîmes.

"We would like you to have tea with us," said Miss Stein.

It was a very welcome invitation. That afternoon big plates of sweet cakes and pots of tea were spread on a huge table in the lobby; Miss Toklas served and did most of the talking, while Miss Stein and I ate.

They were with the American Fund for French Wounded. Driving a car fitted with a truck body, they delivered gifts to French soldiers, many of them serious gas cases, in military hospitals in the three departments of the Gard, Bouches-du-Rhône and Vaucluse. Until recently they had worked out of Perpignan. They were Americans, and their home was in Paris, said Miss Toklas.

"Miss Stein writes," she added.

I had no idea whatsoever of what she wrote, and I didn't ask, though why I didn't I can't today imagine. That was the only specific mention by either of them of Miss Stein's work, though every remaining day of my furlough was spent in their company. If Miss Stein already regarded herself as a genius, as she would claim openly in 1933 in *The Autobiography of Alice B. Toklas,* she was not boasting about it at that time to strangers.

They pumped me, however, for all they were worth. Where was I born, who were my parents, what did my father do, where did I go to college, who were my professors, how did I happen to be in the army, was this my first visit to France, what would I do when the war ended?

One spelled the other, like police grilling a prisoner for hours on end, until they dragged my whole history out of me.

Spread out over ten days, such questions as these, which under almost any other circumstances might have been very irritating, did not strike me as prying or excessively inquisitive. Instead, they had an oddly comforting effect. Here was I for the first time in my young life thousands of miles from my native Massachusetts, and these two kind women managed to put me completely at ease, they made me feel right back at home. I was not in alien Nîmes, I'd just dropped in to visit my favorite aunt: how've you been, what have you been doing, is your work coming on all right, what do you plan to do when you go back?

From the start they made it my vacationtime. And they made it theirs, too, for constant work had induced in them the mood for relaxation. Since they had to run around the country dispensing charity, and I wanted to run around the country sightseeing, Miss Toklas suggested that their jaunts be arranged to fulfill a double purpose. For me that was the grandest charity of all, if only because many Roman and Romanesque monuments were practically inaccessible to anyone depending on railways.

While I now gladly acknowledge that their invitation was the most important event in my experience up to that time, I then regarded it mainly as a bit of uncommon luck; they wanted to do me a good turn and from the bottom of my heart I was grateful. Soldiers were always being entertained; in our base camp in America

9

the ladies of the community had asked us to dinners and sociables and we had attended them, the best intentioned and the most boring affairs in the world. This was different; I was delighted because I foresaw how enjoyable the company of Miss Stein and Miss Toklas would be. I liked them.

Perhaps it must be explained that a little courage was needed for that. An unventuresome, self-conscious New Englander, though he has lived in the town which remembered the recluse Emily Dickinson and has heard of the redoubtable Amy Lowell and her cigars, is still peculiarly unfitted by environment and training, including a classical education, to appreciate the qualities of Miss Stein and Miss Toklas if he must come at them through their unconventional wrappings. They the cosmopolitans never made any effort to conform; I the provincial had made little effort to do anything else.

Compared to this couple, the overalled farmerettes at whom the folks back home were gawping were inconspicuous. Miss Toklas wore a sort of uniform, a skirt and long cloak over it, belted, with baggy, unbuttoned, official-looking pockets like those sported by British officers. Both had helmet-shaped hats, Miss Toklas' over hair clipped short and Miss Stein's over hair which was still long. Miss Stein dressed even more outlandishly, with sandals buckled on over the ankles, a full skirt, knitted vest and shirtwaist with sleeves gathered at the wrists—in the uniforms of Greek Evzones, at least from the hips up, there was something of the same bizarre fashion.

At that time I might have laughed at what I resented thirty years later: one publisher's advertisement, to counter another publisher's picture of attractive Kathleen Winsor, showing Miss Stein and Miss Toklas as firm, foursquare and everlasting as granite, and with a beauty all their own; the underline read:

"Shucks, we've got glamour girls too."

If their costumes were unlike anything a boy would ever encounter on the streets of Boston, Springfield and Amherst, it was nevertheless obvious that they possessed a distinctive style and form. With Miss Toklas the mode, if the word may apply to something so unrelated to modish, was military; in Miss Stein's case it was homely, with no elegance at all, and still somehow regal. Their clothes violated all my notions of what the well dressed woman should wear, yet fitted them to an S and a T.

These ridiculous obstacles to my liking the two women, who were then in their forties, were overcome not because I used my brains but because they used theirs. No one could spend five minutes with them without knowing they were something extra special; if no bell within me rang, as Miss Toklas would later report of her first meetings with the three geniuses she knew, something within me clicked.

To begin with, they were ceaselessly thoughtful, and nothing that could make my furlough more fun was too much bother for them. After that, they were fascinating conversationalists; with equal facility, each one would delve into the field of ideas, and then lighten it gaily with the most pungent personalities, more commonly known as gossip and scandal, and I would have been content to listen uninterruptedly for months.

11

But in addition, once I learned to ignore the oddities in their appearance, I came to appreciate how striking they were. Miss Toklas' dark attractiveness owed much to her sparkle and animation. Miss Stein, I thought and think, had a distinguished and beautiful face, strong, open, molded massively on big, generous lines and planes; it reminded me of eighteen-inch sculpture which mysteriously produces an eighteen-foot effect. The mouth was wide, the complexion weathered, the dark brown eyes mellow and magnetic. Her voice carried easily, and her infectious laughter would sometimes rumble like thunder.

In future years when Miss Stein's writing had achieved an extensive reputation, the people who jeered at it took the further step, I suppose naturally, of jeering at the way she looked. But the weight of evidence is on the other side. Picasso, who as an artist ought to have known, was much attracted to her physically almost a decade before I met her. Some one would observe later that she had a face like Caesar's, and an American author praised her as having the statuesque appeal of a robed nun. When Peggy Bacon made a sketch of her, she called Miss Stein's head as "striking as Stonehenge."

This was of course a game at which two could play, and Miss Stein and Miss Toklas would always be spotting in friends or acquaintances near likenesses to historical figures or personages in paintings. I for instance in a photo taken by Carl Van Vechten had a "really and truly" Lincoln look, said Miss Stein. Picasso, too, though without benefit of photograph, looked like Lincoln; Mildred Aldrich like George Washington, a

French journalist "like a caricature of Uncle Sam made french," Lady Ottoline Morrell like Disraeli, some one else like Disraeli's daughter and some one else like a Goya painting of Queen Maria Luisa on horseback, a landlady in Florence like a lady-in-waiting to Mary Stuart, Marcel Duchamp like a young Norman crusader, Mabel Dodge like the actress Georgia Cayvan, George Moore like a Mellin's Food baby, Avery Hopwood like a lamb and, of course, perhaps the best known comparison and certainly the most trouble making, Madame Matisse like a horse.

3

Because the two women were so out of the ordinary, I was not surprised at the manner in which the rides were suggested. Miss Toklas did not invite me, she "propositioned" me. I was asked to go, or told that I might, under certain specified conditions, every one designed to make the holiday trips as easy and comfortable as possible for Miss Stein. If anything went wrong with the car, I would try to fix it, as my experience with Fords should enable me to. We must always be back at the hotel by nightfall because Miss Stein objected to driving in the dark. I must not get in the way; I would sit on the floor with my feet on the running board so that there would be every inch as much room for Miss Stein as if I were not there.

Of course I agreed happily. I sat on a pillow, half out the open door, my knees up under my chin, and I crowded Miss Toklas but not Miss Stein. Miss Toklas has devoted practically all her adult life to the prevention of any crowding of Gertrude Stein. Alone by themselves, Miss Toklas was "Pussy" and Miss Stein "Lovey" and a deep attachment united them for almost half a century. Miss Toklas determinedly put Miss Stein on a higher level and stayed carefully, even religiously, off it; she deferred, played second fiddle, knew her place.

Their wartime car was christened "Auntie," from a relative of Miss Stein's who "always behaved admirably in emergencies and behaved fairly well most times if she was properly flattered." Miss Stein walked me up to the garage to introduce me to her, one of those spindly autos which take after their real aunt, the buggy. Looking more like an assemblage of parts than one solid piece, it rode high on wooden wheels with bicycle-size tires; a box rather than a hood covered the motor; half of the windshield, which split in the middle horizontally, could be turned up to let in air on a perspiring driver; the mudguards bent up and forward at anything but a rakish angle; the top above the seat was collapsible. In effect, much of the car was collapsible, and Miss Stein and Miss Toklas had their troubles, though on our travels they amounted to nothing more serious than flat tires and boiling radiator.

Across a completely charming countryside where the air had the tang of ripening fruit, and where white, chalky soil burst in brilliant splashes through the vivid, sometimes dazzling green of the foliage, we visited hospitals, beauty spots, monuments, and a battlefield where Caesar's legions had fought. We saw walled Aiguesmortes, which is dug into the edge of mud flats that slither off into the Mediterranean. We marveled at the soaring triumphal arch at ancient Glanum, near St. Rémy. We admired the beautiful Romanesque façade at Saint Gilles. We climbed over the tumbled remains of Les Baux, one of the most picturesque and romantic aspects of western Europe, a mountain peak extended dizzily upward by the dilapidated walls of churches, homes and ramparts; the steep hairpin curves leading to this antique Protestant stronghold were a challenge to the Ford, which steamed, stopped to catch a breath, and steamed onward and upward again. The itinerary included Tarascon, Arles, Avignon, and Orange, the delightful Sainte Gabrielle chapel, and picnic lunches when the mistral didn't blow the plates away or hotel dinners when it did . . . to such gourmets as Miss Stein and Miss Toklas, picnic lunch prepared by Miss Toklas was no anticlimax even to the marvels of the Midi.

Distances of course were short, but then Auntie was a slowpoke. Miss Stein had a scary habit of talking and forgetting about driving. She also had a habit of spoiling Miss Toklas' careful plans; the route to Avignon, for example, was to the right, according to the map, but Miss Stein, still wanting to reach Avignon, preferred the left. Returning once from the Mediterranean, we rumbled along the flat, sea-level roads, jounced across a bridge of boats, guessed wrong at an intersection and, with no kilometre stones to guide us, lost our way and were delayed until after dark. I shinnied up a signpost and scratched a match to read directions.

That night I learned why Miss Toklas had labored to bring us home before sunset; though the headlights showed some one else where we were, they didn't show us what lay right under our three noses. In the course of all our jaunts I learned, too, why Miss Toklas had hedged her invitation about so severely. Openhearted, generous, anxious for me to enjoy the time of my life—which I did—Miss Stein would wait patiently even if I stretched my sightseeing far beyond the limits of her interest, or she would go out of her way gladly to provide me with an extra, unscheduled treat. I had the impression that nothing in the world mattered to her so much as showing me the marvels and beauties of the region. As soon as I began trying obviously not to take advantage of her kindness, she turned the tables on me and put me everlastingly in her debt. Miss Toklas should have addressed her don't-do-this and don't-do-that to Miss Stein, not to me, and I'm sure she was aware of that and also aware that it wouldn't do any good at all.

Every minute of the furlough was an education for this lucky doughboy:

"The Louvre has nothing but nothing to compare with this," Miss Stein declared of the Saint Gilles façade.

"Giving the waiter a fifty-franc note for an eighteen-franc bill is asking him to cheat you," Miss Toklas warned in an Arles restaurant on the only occasion when the dinner was allowed to come out of my thirty-six dollars monthly pay.

"Had you told me you were going to Uzès, I would have written a letter of introduction to la Duchesse d'Uzès," said Miss Stein—and thus I missed seeing the grande dame who was not only mistress to the hounds to a Bourbon pretender but also, significantly, one of

16

the backers of that General Boulanger, the man on the white horse, who raised the last reactionary threat, prior to World War II, to republican France.

Incidents of this sort multiplied, but the days ran out. I told Miss Stein and Miss Toklas good-bye late one afternoon as fall changed to winter and the biting mistral started in earnest to sweep the dust out of the streets of Nîmes. We promised to write, and they gave me their Paris address, 27 rue de Fleurus, destined to become one of the famous literary addresses of the first half of this century. Miss Toklas and I exchanged some letters, and I called on them once in Paris but they were still away. Miss Toklas spelled my name Rodgers, and did for years, just as Miss Stein would later usually write on the envelope W. K. Rodgers and often add a hundred or so to my street number, to the confusion of the postman.

About a year after the war our correspondence ceased. I was certain I should never forget them. I supposed, too, that I might never see them again; in the light of one thing and another that was, happily, as ridiculous a supposition as ever occurred to me.

THEY NATURALLY DID NOT KNOW ABOUT IT THEN

1

ON JULY 27, 1946, Gertrude Stein died in a Paris hospital after an operation for an abdominal tumor already in a hopelessly advanced state of malignancy.

If death had struck in 1917, when I first knew her, she might have received a few lines in a provincial French newspaper, and obituary notices: "Stein, Gertrude, in Nîmes, etc.", in the press of Pittsburgh and San Francisco, but no more. Actually, by 1946, she had caught up with the fame for which she had hungered so ravenously; whatever the public might think of her writings, they had elevated her to a secure position among the leading contemporary celebrities. Innumerable newspapers carried lengthy biographies. The sad word reached me by radio, before Miss Toklas' cable arrived; it was one of those five-minute broadcasts when the most important events of the day are summarized, and on a day full of critical international developments she rated her spot in that brief round-up.

Week after week in the months before and after her death she made the music, book, art or news columns. *Brewsie and Willie,* her account of conversations with GI's, had been published five days before her decease, just in time to feature memorial displays in Fifth Avenue bookstore windows—and almost exactly a year later her estranged brother Leo died in Italy after a similar operation within two weeks of receiving copies of his new book. In the spring of 1946 the Pasadena Playhouse presented Miss Stein's last play, *Yes Is for a Very Young Man,* and there have been extensive negotiations for a Broadway production. The *Selected Writings of Gertrude Stein* was edited by one of her most constant friends, Carl Van Vechten, who in the meantime had undertaken at her request the very considerable task of arranging her unsold manuscripts for posthumous publication. Virgil Thomson composed the music for her last opera, *The Mother of Us All,* successor in homespun to that matchless experiment in cellophane, *Four Saints in Three Acts,* and it was produced before delighted audiences at Columbia University's third annual festival of American music in May; and Thomson conducted a broadcast of *Four Saints.* A Dublin and London house brought out Miss Stein's *First Reader* and printed a special American edition for early 1948. Thornton Wilder, friend of Miss Stein's for fifteen years, edited *Four in America,* and his foreword proved to be one of the most illuminating studies yet made of her position in letters. The Yale Library, which at Wilder's suggestion had become the depository of all her papers, presented a well-attended exhibition of letters, manuscripts and photographs, and they received wide attention in the magazines and newspapers. Shortly before her death Miss Stein wrote me that she had sold book rights to Scandinavia, England, America and other countries and complained because there was nothing more to sell. As I write this, four other books about her are in preparation, one on her as art patron and the rest on her writing.

And that wasn't all. The Metropolitan Museum of Art dispatched two envoys to receive from Miss Toklas Miss Stein's bequest, Picasso's magnificent portrait of her. There were radio talks, and salutes, affectionate if not invariably worshipful, from critics and columnists. Julian Sawyer, her first bibliographer, ardent young apostle with all the earmarks of a cultist, gave a series of lectures about her prose and verse, pages and pages of which, practically impossible to memorize, he neverthe-less recited from memory. On the first anniversary of her death a band of devotees met in the Gotham Book Mart to hear recordings of her voice, a reading by Thornton Wilder, recitations by Sawyer, and a report direct from Paris about Miss Toklas.

Millions of people knew the name of Stein, though of course many associated it vaguely with a kind of literature which can be explained best, as one of them commented with utter condescension and inaccuracy, by the brain tumor to which she succumbed. Millions knew, thanks to widely disseminated news photographs and Carl Van Vechten's masterly camera studies, her force-ful features, deep brow and piercing eyes. Almost as many millions must have known the name of Alice B. Toklas, of whose very existence, however, the two women's friends, among them Henry McBride of the New York *Sun*, had felt it necessary to reassure cynical readers of the Toklas *Autobiography* less than fifteen years before.

It had not been enough to be a genius. Before death overtook her, she could exult, and she did in public and private, that she was a "celebrity," a word recurring again and again in *Everybody's Autobiography*.

There was glory enough, certainly, to satisfy even an abnormal appetite. But these fat years must compensate for the long, heartbreaking lean years which preceded them. Even as late as the thirties some London editors were rejecting her manuscripts in terms like these:

"I really cannot publish these curious studies."

"I cannot read your M.S. three or four times. Not even one time. Only one look, only one look is enough. Hardly one copy would sell here. Hardly one. Hardly one."

"I have only read a portion of it because I found it perfectly useless to read further as I did not understand any of it."

From 1930 to 1932, when a very gratifying triumph lay just ahead, Miss Stein and Miss Toklas were obliged to become publishers themselves, and under the "Plain Edition" imprint they brought out *Lucy Church Amiably, Before the Flowers of Friendship Faded Friendship Faded, How to Write, Operas and Plays* and *Matisse Picasso and Gertrude Stein*. Except for reprints of *Three Lives*, originally published at the author's own expense; except for some imported copies

21

of *The Making of Americans;* and except for a five-dollar de luxe edition of *Useful Knowledge,* Miss Stein was fifty-nine years old before any regular American publisher was willing to invest his own money and indorse with his own name any of her full-length works. Even then it was the Toklas *Autobiography;* since it was couched in more traditional English, for theoretically it was written by Miss Toklas, and since it was anyway a rousing good yarn about the playful, colorful and sinful Left Bank, its publication involved little financial or literary risk.

If Miss Stein is blamed for boasting in the 1940s, when she had a lot to boast about, she must be credited with exemplary modesty in the 1910s, when on the face of it she had plenty to be modest about. Who had heard her name? Who had read her books? Who, she must have asked herself many times, was ever likely to? Twenty years later she recalled that World War I Yanks "naturally did not know about it then."

I had been one of many, consequently, and if my ignorance of the identity of the remarkable woman I had met by chance was inexcusable, it was still explicable.

2

Before the first World War, Miss Stein had written the two works which I regard as her prime contribution to modern letters: *Three Lives* and *Tender Buttons,* respectively a little step away from traditional writing and a complete about-face from it. Her rue de Fleurus salon was becoming the place in Paris at which it was important to be seen. She had the sort of friends and acquaintances considered the indubitable mark of success: the Infanta Eulalia, Roger Fry, Clive Bell, Mildred Aldrich, Jacob Epstein, Gino Severini, Pablo Picasso, Henri Matisse, Jo Davidson, Francis Picabia, Mabel Dodge [Luhan], André Gide, Carl Van Vechten, John Reed, Avery Hopwood, Gertrude Atherton, Serge Lifar, Bernard Berenson, Wyndham Lewis . . . the list could go on for pages.

But she was still as completely unknown to the public as she had been throughout her uneventful childhood before she and her brother Leo settled in the Paris apartment which she and Miss Toklas left only in 1938.

The unique career, which for half a century threatened not to blossom out into any career at all, began in Allegheny City, now a part of Pittsburgh, where Gertrude Stein was born in 1874 on the third of February, the month which, as she herself inevitably pointed out, was previously notable only for the birthdays of Washington and Lincoln. But she claimed no less for Miss Toklas, whose birthday, she wrote me, is "the 30 of April, she comes right in with the king of Spain and Hitler and Daisy Fellowes [a friend], horoscopically speaking it's a mixed bag, of which we have the Pearl."

Miss Stein was the youngest and Michael the oldest of the five children, all natives of the same city, who lived to grow up. The others were Leo, Bertha and Simon. Simon eventually became a gripman on San Francisco cable cars, and Bertha was married. Bertha and Simon, Miss Stein pretended, were a "little simpleminded."

The fact that Leo was endowed with tastes comparable to those of Gertrude and Michael was not enough to maintain a friendship, and anyway, who wants to live with a brother, or who with a sister, all the years of their lives?

"You have no idea how dumb she was," Leo once remarked in the hearing of Samuel Putnam, he reported in *Paris Was Our Mistress,* and though no admirer of Miss Stein's, Putnam reflected that her college and university record contradicted this opinion. Leo himself denied the quotation specifically, but the estrangement persisted for thirty-five years, after about as long a period of intimate association. A comparison of his writing with hers indicates that their minds worked in somewhat the same ways, if often in contrary directions; some of the mannerisms of his prose resemble hers, and they shared many intellectual interests.

In one respect, however, the one was indistinguishable from the other: the sister's opinion of herself was not a bit more exalted than the brother's opinion of himself. In his recent book, *Appreciation: Painting, Poetry and Prose,* he told how he painted a cubist picture before the cubists, how the great contemporary artists looked to him for advice. After some of this advice, looked for or not, proffered to Picasso, the puzzled painter sadly asked Gertrude why, since Leo had assured him he drew as well as Raphael, he didn't let him alone so that he could keep at it. A Stein was a Stein was a Stein, obviously, though there was less Stein in Michael than in the other two and none of it showed in Gertrude in the first days when I knew her.

She would decide she was a genius and Leo was not, so "little by little we never met again." When I imprudently asked her how she liked what seemed to me his admirable book, *The ABC of Aesthetics,* she replied shortly:

"I've never read it."

Leo believed in letting sleeping sisters lie. The only public statements of his with which I am familiar show him embarrassedly deploring, not the rift, but the advertisement of it, and intimates of his insist he never uttered a word revealing that he held any grudge against the more renowned Gertrude.

He was only one of the countless relatives and friends with whom Miss Stein quarreled. Discovering early in life that "quarreling is to me very interesting," she indulged in it on some occasions as a child might indulge in candy. In later years when she and I were exchanging letters in which to my great distress she criticized severely the current trends of democratic government, I prefaced a couple of my objections with the to me comforting reflection that though our ideas seemed far apart we apparently were moving toward the same position from opposite directions, and might really be in agreement at bottom. She answered bluntly that this was this and that was that and that it didn't matter at all whether we agreed. To tell the truth, we did not agree, and abstractly speaking it did not matter, but I expected that a quarrel would hurt and Miss Stein expected no such thing.

She always enjoyed meeting anyone once, when she would make up her mind as to whether he merited a second encounter. After she became famous and people from the distant past began to remember her with a new found love and importunate visits, she proposed, humorously, a paid newspaper announcement to the effect that she did not care now to see persons whom she had not seen for fifteen years. She wanted auld acquaintance to be forgot.

Many quarrels were forced on her, not merely by hostile critics of her person and her writing but also by lukewarm friends, and if she enjoyed entering the ring, she was also well trained for it. An artist expressed the wish one day that she make the acquaintance of a certain woman. Miss Stein wondered why. It would be a great help, of course, the artist replied. Miss Stein asked, a help to whom? To you, Miss Stein, he said. She didn't believe it, and she finally informed him flatly that, if he wanted to bring about the introduction because he expected that it would lead to the sale of some of his paintings to the other woman, she, Miss Stein, would permit the introduction. And, as she frequently wrote, if not not.

She was not the only quarrelsome Stein. Her mother and the wife of her father's brother could not get along together, and so Daniel, her father, split with the brother with whom he had carried on a business in Pennsylvania and traveled off with his share of the money and his family to Vienna. When he returned to this country, Mrs. Stein moved her brood to Paris, and Gertrude lived there for the first time when she was four and five years old. French friends, French theatre and art, and packages from Paris with clothes, furs and perfumes would

26

keep the pleasant memory of that visit fresh in San Francisco, where they later joined the father.

There in street railways Daniel devised an ambitious plan for a merger; after his death Michael sold the idea and so impressed the parent company with his ability that he was named manager of the entire trolley system. He retired at an early age to live on his laurels and his modest savings. Due to his acumen, the Stein fortune was large enough to leave Gertrude "reasonably poor," as she described it. She had a dependable income. It was so small that she paid no tax on it, but it made life in France possible and even comfortable, though it would not have sufficed in the United States. Above all, it gave her security; she could travel, patronize young painters, entertain, and go very leisurely, as she needed to do, about the job of writing. Thanks to the merger and to Michael, she could afford to wait until almost sixty to earn her own way, or part of it, with the Toklas *Autobiography;* only then could she indulge in what she exuberantly called the "sudden splendid spending of money."

A photograph taken in Vienna when she was three or four years old shows her with a broad sash around her middle, a rather dour, hostile face and the fingers of one hand clenched almost to a fist. As Miss Stein was not an ordinary woman, she could hardly have been an ordinary child, and this picture may serve as an index to what she was in California.

What she refers to more than once as her solitary existence in Oakland must have been psychological

27

rather than physical, since she was reared in the midst of a large family. Her acknowledged need of social contacts in her twenties and thirties presumably indicates that she already had suffered for lack of them. Furthermore, by her own account, books meant a great deal while she was still a youngster, and her fare was much beyond her years. The normal adolescent girl, busy with playmates, games, clothes, parties, school lessons, does not read "Wordsworth, Scott and other poets, Bunyan's Pilgrim's Progress, a set of Shakespeare with notes, Burns, Congressional Records, encyclopedias"; she does not "absorb" Shakespeare nor pore over *Clarissa Harlowe*, Fielding, Smollett, and a "tremendous amount of history." At seventeen, when she went to Baltimore, she found life among her mother's relatives animated and interesting, a contrast obviously to what it had been before.

Still staying close to brother Leo, the Harvard student, she went to Radcliffe. The mere fact of college enrollment in the 1890s distinguished her from the vast majority of her countrywomen, and her career there further emphasized the differences. Though she professed to "dislike the abnormal, it is so obvious" and to prefer the normal as "so much more simply complicated," yet at least as much as any other young woman of her day she abhorred a beaten path. She was not cut out of the same cloth as the rest of them, and maybe her consciousness of that induced her shyness.

For the first time stepping out into the world on her own, she made a mark in it almost at once. Under Münsterberg's direction she and a Harvard student experimented in automatic writing, and her summary of the laboratory findings constituted her first published work. In one of William James's classes, she wrote on her final examination paper merely that she did not feel like writing; her understanding teacher approved, gave her the highest mark in his course, and is said to have called her the most brilliant woman student he ever had.

He advised her to study either philosophy or psychology, and she chose the latter, again the less customary decision, the one that would not have been made by most of her contemporaries. Since she needed medical training for this purpose, she entered Johns Hopkins medical school in 1900, but by 1903 was thoroughly bored, or acted it, and would not study. Most of her professors, willing to overlook her erratic nature for the sake of her indubitable intelligence, passed her, but one who preferred the plodding type kept her from being graduated. He took the pains, however, to point out that a summer course would enable her to get a degree. She rose to the occasion, as she had invariably done before, picked the spectacular alternative and abandoned medicine.

In other words, Gertrude Stein already was directing attention repeatedly to Gertrude Stein. Where the limelight was brightest, she took her stance there immovably. She called down the lightning flash upon herself.

The thunder followed after, for the same accusation has been brought against her by those who, irritated by her writing, try to dismiss her as a publicity hound. The same charge may be leveled, however at great creative spirits in other centuries and climates. Poe gambled, drank and whored as testimony to the manhood he had not yet achieved, and Tolstoy bowed backward like a clown to impress his parents' guests, shaved his head to shock his family, and jumped out of a window to demonstrate that he alone in the world could fly.

According to the authoritative Miss Toklas, the limelight really held no attraction for Miss Stein in the early years. We must conclude then that chance placed her in those successive conspicuous positions, which soon proved so agreeable that eventually she couldn't bear to be anywhere else, as admittedly she couldn't.

In either case, Miss Stein's detractors overreach themselves when they claim that, since she was a show-off, she couldn't be a genius. It does not follow, from the desire of Poe and Tolstoy to be conspicuous, that they wrote gibberish. It does not follow, from Miss Stein's identical desire, whether it appeared early or late, that she wrote gibberish, either.

If you win fame at twenty or twenty-five, you don't have blatantly to state your own case. If however you wait until you're sixty, you are obliged to justify your own efforts. A person who works four or five decades without getting even the gold watch or the banquet tendered to any fifty-year conductor, hardware clerk or janitor is either bright enough to know what he's doing and demand the watch and banquet as his just reward, or stupid since as far as he knows he has wasted his life. Miss Stein might have been ridiculed for asserting she was wasting her life, but can't be honestly for asserting she was not.

The war which had deposited Miss Stein and Miss Toklas in Nîmes had caught them at its outbreak in England. John Lane wanted to publish *Three Lives* to celebrate its fifth birthday in the original privately-printed edition, and the two women crossed the Channel to sign the contract in the summer of 1914.

They went to Lockridge for a weekend with the Whiteheads, Alfred the philosopher being one of the three, including Miss Stein and painter Pablo Picasso, of whom Miss Toklas is made by Miss Stein to say in the *Autobiography* that "only three times in my life have I met a genius and each time a bell within me rang."

Because of Germany's attack, they extended their stay to six weeks, and tried to relieve their worry about the enemy's overwhelming thrust deep into their beloved France with lunches, dinners and teas attended by A. E. Housman, Lytton Strachey, Bertrand Russell and others. On returning to Paris, where Mrs. Whitehead accompanied them to deliver to her son North, a combatant in that old-fashioned, easy-going war, an overcoat she was afraid he needed, Miss Stein immediately dispatched manuscripts to safety in America. Carl Van Vechten stored them for her and continued to do so over the years.

After some months of Zeppelin alarms, and of farewells to friends entering some branch of service, they visited Palma de Majorca to "forget the war a little." Once more back in Paris, Miss Stein learned, or partly learned, to drive an automobile, with artist William Cook teaching her in an old Battle-of-the-Marne taxi. Her interest awakened one day by the sight of an American Fund car, she volunteered, bought a Ford, ventured on a few trial trips in and about Paris, set off brashly for the Midi, and arrived at last in Nîmes, with Miss Toklas of course.

The French government, in honoring them later with citations for their relief work, seemed to me unusually perspicacious, for a government, in defining Miss Toklas' assistance as sans relâche, or without relaxing. That defines her exactly; at home and away, she never did let up, she never stopped.

At first glance, the Miss Toklas whom I first saw in 1917 and last saw in 1947, was and has remained a little stooped, somewhat retiring and self-effacing. She doesn't sit in a chair, she hides in it; she doesn't look at you, but up at you; she is always standing just half a step outside the circle. She gives the appearance, in short, not of a drudge, but of a poor relation, some one invited to the wedding but not to the wedding feast.

But in the first moment after the first glance, the impact of her wit, her tonic acidity, and her amazing vitality makes itself felt unmistakably. Though you assumed you would devote all your attention to Miss Stein, you found yourself obliged to direct a generous share of it to Miss Toklas, even against her wishes.

She is the sort of person who has always looked fairly well along in years, to me, yet she must have been a fun-loving girl if we may judge by Harriet Levy's brief revelations in her memoirs about San Francisco where Miss Toklas was born. When Miss Toklas went to Paris, with Miss Levy as her companion, she was supplied with a letter to Michael Stein, whose family she had known in her native city. At Michael's she met Gertrude.

That was a crucial moment for both of them, for Miss Toklas who had left behind her some dull and wearing years, and for the absorbed, aloof Miss Stein, already in appearance a sort of priestess, more than thirty years old, prepared at least subconsciously to break away from the fond though evidently domineering Leo.

Miss Stein and Miss Toklas began to go out to art shows in the afternoon and the theatre at night. The acquaintance grew into friendship, and when about 1913 Leo moved to a permanent home in Italy, where he had spent many pleasant months with his sister, Miss Toklas and Miss Stein were left alone together in the rue de Fleurus apartment. Later they would travel to Italy, and to Spain and Majorca and in the summer out into the French countryside. They developed into a perfect pair, each supplying what the other lacked, like the Jack Spratts.

One way to rile Miss Toklas, and one out of many, is to tell her you suspect her touch in the Stein genius, though it is of course a quite natural suspicion for which Miss Toklas should blame, not her admirers, but Miss Stein herself, author of the Toklas *Autobiography;* and for that matter, the better you knew them, the more you wondered whose light was being hidden under whose bushel. Their likes and dislikes did not always coincide, but Miss Toklas very subtly distinguished between potential friends and foes and was adept at anticipating the time when the ones would be metamorphosed into the others; Miss Stein got bored with people and dropped them, but in this there was certainly more than just a touch of Toklas.

When the sedan they later owned was full, Miss Toklas took a back seat, and she took a back seat figuratively, too. A photographer in search of a series of pictures of Miss Stein engaged in some activity suggested that she unpack her suitcase, but was told that Miss Toklas always performed that chore; he suggested that she telephone, but was told Miss Toklas always did that, too. Miss Stein formally identified Miss Toklas as her "secretary" who "struggled with my tenses and genders," and she did type her manuscripts, or as Miss Stein said "ticktack" them, and also run the house, serve as business manager, even for a time as printer and publisher, and general factotum. That was the actual and official relationship, but an infinitely closer and profounder tie united them.

As I recall the wonderful furlough in Nîmes, I realize that I learned more about my friends than I suspected. It was, however, they who really turned the holiday into a lesson by their insistent direct questions. They puzzled me, and I wondered what the explanation was. Theirs was the kind of curiosity, perhaps, that killed a cat. Or they wanted to be certain, before associating with me, that I was a proper person. Or, less complaisantly, they patterned themselves on the aged Goethe who, pestered by worshipful visitors, avoided their stupid questions by asking the questions himself. Or, more charitably, as I appreciated how hard and how success-fully they tried to give me a good time, they were sufficiently women of the world to realize that no one is quite so happy as when he is invited to talk about himself.

Twenty years later, without a word to refresh her memory, Miss Stein reported the main facts about me accurately in *Everybody's Autobiography*. By that time, of course, I understood. It had been wrong to suppose they were not interested, for in fact they were, genuinely, though less for my sake than for theirs.

It was the difference between a gossip and a novelist, or at least a novelist like Miss Stein. While a genius is one who takes infinite pains, he also in part is one who possesses an infinite storehouse of facts, or "one who is one at one and at the same time telling and listening to anything or everything," as Miss Stein expressed it in *Narration*. The inquisition to which she submitted me pointed directly, I would appreciate later, to the method she developed for that one-thousand-page literary monument, *The Making of Americans*, which she started in 1906 and finished in 1908.

Not published until 1925, *The Making of Americans* was for many critics a grand opportunity for the making of wisecracks. When Miss Stein wrote, for example, about there "coming to be an ending of the beginning of the history of the Hersland family," it was relegated to the comic page, though Britain's wartime Prime Minister rated page one for a phrase not too dissimilar. Exasperated readers, perfectly content to accept *Lear*, *The Divine Comedy* and *Athalie* without asking whether

Shakespeare, Dante or Racine talked the way they wrote, insisted indignantly on knowing whether Miss Stein talked the way she wrote.

As a matter of fact, she both wrote and talked exactly the way she thought. It was a man's "bottom nature" for which she probed with such painstaking ardor, just as she had been concerned inordinately with her own "bottom nature," or what she called "what made me myself inside me."

She projected "every kind of a history of everyone who ever can or is or was or will be living." It was an essential part of her task that she should be the indefatigable investigator. Her genius was to grub. I in Nîmes, since I was handy, became just another exhibit; I was turned inside out and picked to pieces as a potential case history.

Out of such laborious methods as this, by inching forward and inching back, by roundabout and redundancy and not hitting the nail on the head, by inversion, augmentation and diminution, she achieved what some annoyed people have charged is an equally laborious description: "A man in his living has many things inside him. He has in him his feeling himself important to himself inside him, he has in him his way of beginning."

She attributed the change in her way of writing to a change in her way of living:

"I am beginning to like conversation, I used not to like conversation at all, and social living, and so going on and on I am needing always I am needing something to give to me completely successful diversion to give me enough stimulation to keep me completely going on being going on living."

That kept her being going on writing. In one of her American lectures she lamented the contrast between the prolonged process of acquiring a complete conception of an individual and the eventually spontaneous awareness. That is, a person becomes known in two ways, first bit by bit and then all at once in his totality . . . very much as an abstractionist feels around his subject plane by plane and then of a sudden produces his painting. That was a "terrible trouble to me," Miss Stein confessed, and it has been no less to quizzical readers encountering a statement of the problem and her solution of it for the first time in literature.

We must remember that that was the first decade of this century. Taft was headed for the presidency, the North Pole was discovered, and Eliot filled a five-foot bookshelf for us. Theodore Dreiser and Sherwood Anderson were beginning to write, and Upton Sinclair gave us *The Jungle.* But on most library shelves you found *To Have and to Hold, The Virginians, Graustark, The Clansman, The Hound of the Baskervilles, The Little Shepherd of Kingdom Come.*

Wherever *The Making of Americans* belongs, it is not in this romantic category. It is a somewhat disguised account of the author's relatives on father's and mother's sides, the Dehnings in Bridgepoint [Baltimore] and the Herslands in Gossols [Oakland, California]. It's a story that is going on keeping continuing, like the interminable questioning in Nîmes. It is not Miss Stein writing, but Miss Stein and her friends and acquaintances being. It is not characters introduced, as is said of the people in the typical novel, but characters introducing themselves, appearing faintly in the distance, growing larger, clearer, more sharply outlined; they formulate their own questions, laboriously, painfully, with a "terrible trouble," and supply their own exhaustive answers. Piecemeal and revelation coincide.

Back in 1917 both Miss Stein and Miss Toklas had seemed to me extremely reticent, almost as if they were sworn to conceal everything. There were of course many hints of their special interests in art and literature, and their extraordinary familiarity with those fields. But when I left, though I could surmise from the deference shown Miss Stein by Miss Toklas that she was a person of vast importance at least in Miss Toklas' eyes, I still knew nothing about the books already written or the paintings already chosen and purchased. Of course, I should have realized that all I wanted to know was revealed by the questions put to me; when I was asked a great deal, I was thereby told a great deal. Even at her most sociable, Miss Stein remained the active creative writer.

$\mathcal{P}$ARIS IS MY HOME TOWN

1

AFTER OUR NIMES meeting, the name of Gertrude Stein in print caught my eye for the first time in the twenties, but I do not remember exactly when. I might have run across *Three Lives* but didn't. I didn't see other pieces in the experimental magazine *transition*, or stray items in the New York *Sun* and the *Life* magazine of that day. There remains now only the memory of Miss Stein's photograph in a sepia rotogravure section of some Sunday paper.

By 1929, however, the avant-garde writer and art collector had been positively identified as my wartime acquaintance. In that year, I stopped at the rue de Fleurus apartment in Paris to pay my respects, and learned from the concierge that Miss Stein and Miss Toklas were out of the city. Announcements of the forthcoming *Autobiography of Alice B. Toklas* appeared in 1932, and in extracts from it in *The Atlantic Monthly*, I recognized not only Miss Stein and Miss Toklas but myself in an incident concerning an "american ambulance boy . . . who had gone off to visit a waterfall."

Between the autumn of 1933, when the *Autobiography* was published, and the winter of 1933–34, when the premiere of *Four Saints* sent New York and other music critics swarming to the Avery Memorial Theatre of the Hartford museum, I summoned up my nerve and wrote a letter. Covering both sides of many pages, it left Miss Stein practically nothing to ask questions about. Hoping to be considered as more than just another ex-doughboy, I confessed that I had written and rewritten the letter to render it worthy of her, and added that a novel of mine had been published. They were two errors in judgment, though happily not serious; I was to learn that Miss Stein preferred doughboys and GI's to writers, and that while she sometimes cut her own work a little, she rarely changed a word once it was down on paper.

She replied promptly:

"My dear Kiddie:

"We always called you that you were so young and tender in those days. I don't know that you knew that we called you so, but we did. It was nice hearing from you and they were nice days . . . Do you remember those cigarettes called Darlings with which you used to supply us . . . It all does not seem long ago at all. The waterfall was I believe a very small waterfall indeed, so you said. Do you remember we used to look out on the map for beauty spots, and make our duty coincide with them. The best of wishes to you always and write again. Miss Toklas will write you too very soon . . ."

Several months later, early in the spring of 1934, I

visited Paris again for the Daumier exhibitions in the Musée de l'Orangerie and the Bibliothèque Nationale and to see Miss Stein and Miss Toklas before they left to spend the summer in Bilignin.

"My dear Rodgers," Miss Toklas had addressed me on note paper bearing the much quoted device, "Rose is a rose is a rose is a rose":

"Miss Stein will have told you what real pleasure we are having in your reappearance—and how often we asked each other regularly over the years if you had disappeared for ever . . . We usually leave Paris early in the last week of April but this year it will be a week later. Will you let us know as soon as soon as you know when you are to reach Paris and what your address will be— then we will be able to more easily arrange our meeting."

Calling at the rue de Fleurus, I found them again, the big and the little, the slow and the quick, the oracle and the guardian. Sitting in the poorly lighted salon, the walls of which were lined from floor to ceiling with modern paintings only dimly seen, we talked about the opera in Hartford, the Midi, Nîmes, our hotel there and the brunette who inherited it and now operated it and a blonde who had proved to be a spy for the Germans. In short, we groped our way leisurely toward the intimacy we had once enjoyed.

Of the many Americans who met Miss Stein during that first war, only a few apparently felt drawn back to her, or nourished a constant longing to hunt her out again. This seemingly successful writer struck me, of course, bitten with the desire to become a writer myself, as a most enviable person. But regardless of her books and her phenomenal foresight in art, there was something magnetic and compelling about her. I liked her, that was all; I liked her. I liked Miss Toklas, too, though I was a little afraid of Miss Toklas, and still am. I was never afraid of Miss Stein.

That afternoon, then, was a grand reunion, an old-home day to me, and it pleases me to think it assumed the same significance for them. The resumption of a lapsed acquaintance is arduous; you dash forward here, encounter an uncharted obstacle, retreat quickly and begin all over again. It can become embarrassing, but the dangers are nothing compared to the rewards. The war, so deep in the past, could be discussed comfortably even by people for whom it had provided some uncomfortable moments. We had tea, as in Nîmes, and laughed heartily over little things, and gazed in absorption at one another.

They looked just as they had before; to me, they have always looked the same, as if my fond eyes growing older adjusted themselves to my friends growing older. They seemed unchanged in bulk, outline and detail, with no more stoop, no wrinkles, no diminution in their energy. Miss Stein's hands, for instance, were just as I remembered them: large, firm, usually still, and all of a piece, hands rather than hands-with-fingers, for her fingers appeared to lack separate articulation. It was as if she wore mittens instead of gloves.

There was one difference: Miss Stein's hair, which looked black but was dark brown with a walnut tinge, was cut short. Miss Toklas, who had cut her own just before I first met them, did the job on Miss Stein's, snipping off the braids on a Saturday night and spending hours Sunday trimming it closer and closer to the head. Miss Stein did not leave the house during the day simply because she couldn't. In the evening, an unexpected visit from Sherwood Anderson exposed her to the test she might have preferred to postpone.

Anderson was in the apartment, settled in the salon and being entertained by Miss Toklas when Miss Stein's anxious voice was heard from an inner room:

"What shall I wear?"

"What do you mean," Miss Toklas demanded, "what shall you wear?"

"On my head!"

Anderson asked what was the matter, but before it could be explained, Miss Stein entered. To her relief he was all admiration and he became forthwith the first of several hundred people to liken her to a monk. Some religious quality about her unadorned habiliments brought to mind not so much a nun as a monk. There was something sexless about her, too, a kind of dynamic neuter. She was a robe surmounted by a head, no more carnal than a portly abbot.

Picasso's momentary alarm at the changed coiffure, and then his remark, after studying the woman whose portrait he had painted, that it was still all there, have been recorded. To prove how acute an observer he was, Miss Toklas explains that he discovered a difference when he first glimpsed her, with her hat on, three large rooms away. "Picasso could see around corners," Miss Toklas claims.

On their last Saturday in Paris that spring, they

gave a dinner attended by Count François d'Aiguy, Countess Diane d'Aiguy, who promised to show me the apartment where Virgil Thomson composed the music for *Four Saints*, and Mrs. William Aspenwal Bradley, whose husband was Miss Stein's literary agent. If I did not remember how tiny the dining room was, with everyone backed up to the wall except where the door opened into the kitchen, I would swear many more guests were there, for it was lively and animated.

Others arrived later, for coffee which a maid served under Miss Toklas' watchful supervision. Among them were a girl from Wellesley, as goggle-eyed as I must have been, an art dealer and a protégé with sketchbooks filled with drawings which Miss Stein thought "had something"; Mildred Weston, whose verse was appearing in *The New Yorker*, and several strangers, mostly men.

Conversation bounced around at a merry clip from one topic and one group to another. In one corner it was the young artist and his sketches; in another, affectionate remembrances of the painter Alfred Maurer; in another, the possibility of May Day riots; in another, life in Bilignin and near-by Culoz, home of the d'Aiguys; and in another, poetry. As the only one present who had attended the premiere of *Four Saints*, I had a set speech in praise of it, delivered now in French and now in English to every guest.

Miss Stein reminded me of the poet Verhaeren, who said that the only writing of any interest to him was his own. In *Everybody's Autobiography* Miss Stein would declare: "There is no use going to see a thing if you have not written it no use at all, anyway that is the way I

44

feel about it." So now in her salon, every time I repeated my laudatory remarks about her opera, she stood beaming at my elbow and listened.

2

Freshly returned from London in 1937, Miss Stein wrote me: "London and Paris have changed characters, it is London that is gay and Paris that is somber, too much work and no play can make Jack a dull boy but too much play makes Jack a dismal boy."

But for all the Gerald Bernerses, Cecil Beatons, John Lanes, Alfred Whiteheads and London's gaiety in general, Miss Stein would not have considered for a moment swapping it for her beloved Paris . . . "America is my country and Paris is my home town," she claimed. For anyone who visited Paris the first time while still a wide-eyed, impressionable child, it immediately exerted a tremendous appeal; for Miss Stein, who became familiar with its sights, sounds and smells, its black-aproned schoolchildren, its narrow alleys and broad boulevards and beautifully kept parks when she was little more than an infant, the appeal became irresistible. She adopted the city as her permanent home several years after leaving Johns Hopkins; she wrote *Paris France* as a heartfelt tribute, and her inscription in my French copy of the book, which was printed in 1941, reads in part: "All about our dear France." The place crept into the Stein blood, for brother Leo lived with her there in the early years, and so did brother Michael, and Michael's son settled in Paris.

After Pearl Harbor she wrote me: "The first days of the attack of the Japs was pretty awful, Alice and I were pretty done up, it does not seem that it would be worse than an attack on France but I do suppose that after all one's native land is more one's native land than any other native land."

But it required such moments of crisis to shake her allegiance, since just before her complaints about somber Paris, she was telling me: "Paris I do not know why but this year Paris is its nice old self and everybody knows everybody and everybody is liking it, and painting is once more a subject, Paris is never quite itself unless painting is its subject." In *What Are Masterpieces* she defined it in part: "It is not what France gave you but what it did not take away from you that was important," and in *Paris France* she declared: "Writers ought to have two countries, the one to which they belong and the one in which they actually live." It was less distracting to write in English among people who did not speak it, according to her experience, and of course Paris was much cheaper.

Fernande Olivier, living with Picasso when Gertrude and Leo Stein met the then completely unknown painter, describes brother and sister thus:

"He, looking like a professor, bald, with gold-rimmed glasses. Long beard with ruddy lights [just as Picasso painted him], cunning glance. A big, stiff body, with peculiar poses, with abbreviated gestures. The true type of German-American Jew.

"She, fat, short, massive, beautiful head, strong, with noble features, accentuated, regular, intelligent eyes, seeing clearly, spiritually. Her mind clear and lucid. Masculine, in her voice, in all her walk . . .

"Both were dressed in chestnut-colored corduroy, wearing sandals after the fashion of Raymond Duncan, whose friends [and neighbors] they were. Too intelligent to care about ridicule, too sure of themselves to bother about what other people thought, they were rich and he wanted to paint. She was a doctor, wrote, had been complimented by Wells and was not a little proud of it."

The rue de Fleurus was not one of the oldest parts of Paris, and the Steins were already settled there before the boulevard Raspail was cut through. But it was conveniently located, a couple of minutes from the Luxembourg gardens, on one side, and on the other the Dôme and Rotonde, meeting place for expatriates, though the Steins rarely frequented cafés. As Miss Stein exulted in *Paris France*, "anywhere one lives is interesting and beautiful." The servant, Hélène, ran the household on eight francs a day. With only studio and living quarters, they were cramped. But they were having the time of their young lives and as long as they had walls to hang paintings on, they didn't need much space in between.

Those who scorn Stein the writer are obliged by historical fact to accept Stein the collector, for the pictures picked almost fifty years ago by her alone, or sometimes with Leo, today fill the art magazines, draw the largest crowds to galleries and museums, and fetch the highest prices. The dealer Vollard was endowed with a similar "flair," to quote Fernande though the word does less than justice to that mysterious and remarkable pre-perception, but how many others in her generation exercised her unerring judgment?

Visiting exhibitions and studios, walking her dog, writing her books and talking were Miss Stein's principal preoccupations as described in the Toklas *Autobiography*. The happiest and most exciting times were at her own apartment, and here we refer again to Mme. Olivier, of all witnesses the one least familiar to American readers. Fernande herself, who as Miss Stein described her was "tall . . . very very beautiful with a marvelous complexion," owed her introduction to these soirées to Picasso. She acknowledged that Miss Stein was Picasso's friend rather than hers; and Miss Toklas in the *Autobiography* called her "one of the wives of geniuses with whom I have sat." She would be succeeded by Eve, and eventually by Madame Olga Picasso, the dancer, and she regretted that, "faithful companion of his years of want, I didn't manage to be his companion in prosperous times." But while it lasted it was gay, gay at the Closerie des Lilas where the evening affairs inaugurated by Paul Fort were attended by carefree, young Pablo Picasso, Alfred Jarry, Guillaume Apollinaire, Georges Braque and others, and gay at the Steins' where she saw Pierre Rocher, Max Jacob, Georges Rouault, Elie Nadelmann, Henri Matisse and many others out of the pages of the *Who's Who* of that decade and this, too.

Fernande goes on: "At nine o'clock the crowd was so big that it spread through the apartment, the studio being too small. Mixture of artists, Bohemians, bourgeois, especially foreigners. The spectacle of all these people grouped differently but all discussing art or literature was curious . . .

"The hosts were pleasantly busy with each group, but they were more especially attached to their two great men, Matisse and Picasso."

Alfred Stieglitz distinguished between the hosts, however. He said that one evening he listened to Leo for three hours and during the same three hours looked with admiration at the silent Gertrude.

3

Miss Stein once lamented that the public showed more curiosity about her than about her work. She didn't object to being seen, but she wanted primarily to be read. It's not a surprising complaint, because in some respects she was regarded as an oddity rather than a personage. If people had known her first, I am sure she would have turned them avidly to her works. Encountering the books first, people were driven to seek the explanation for what they did not understand in the person.

"If I could meet Miss Stein, I'm sure I'd like her," readers often declared, but then they behaved toward the prose as they would never have dreamed of behaving toward her. They approached her books familiarly, with a pat on the back or a chuck under the chin. They cried "Hi-ya Gert!" to *Tender Buttons* and *The Making of Americans*, and particularly to *Four Saints*.

A perfumed air of chi-chi pervaded the famous premiere in Hartford, and the fashionable audience divided its attention between the stage and the fashionable audience. If Connecticut valley society and the New York visitors were thrilled, it was not only because of Stein and Thomson but also because the best people sponsored the event and held pre- and post-performance cocktail parties and suppers, and many tickets to the theatre were bought in the hope they meant admission to the right houses.

The public can't be blamed too much, for the sponsors themselves encouraged the notion that the occasion would be social as well as operatic. To be sure, they had bills to meet, and they knew that a circus is guaranteed to pack a house while a serious experiment in music and drama is not.

Miss Stein was no playboy, and never mistook snickers and publicity for applause and fame. The savage strictures of a Clifton Fadiman, who called her smartly though incorrectly the "Mama of Dada," did her cause less harm than the enthusiastic praise of some grinning indorsees. Some people attended the opera because they counted on boasting, if it was adjudged worth while, that they had attended; some went out of the kind of curiosity that always dogged Miss Stein a little and her works a little more.

Though I hinted at this state of affairs, Miss Stein did not care to discuss it with me, or did not care to discuss it, period. From the perspective of the dark and cramped rue de Fleurus apartment, where all the hubbub had originated, such niceties must have seemed inconsequential; no matter who the artist is, he is bound to be blinded for a while after he steps from his isolated studio into the bright light. Receiving not merely reviews but eulogies both in Hartford and a couple of weeks later when the company moved to New York, Miss Stein was naturally delighted with her success and unconcerned about the contradictory reasons for it.

The opera was a hit; a succès d'estime, the composer's friends could rightly cry, a succès de scandale, the librettist's foes could falsely charge. Even in distant Paris Miss Stein could hear her compatriots quoting, with whatever tone of voice mattered little, "Pigeons on the grass alas . . . How many saints are there in it . . . Saint Therese not interested . . . It makes it well fish."

These usual words in unusual contexts led to accusations that Miss Stein was crazy, was trying desperately to attract attention, was doing the pen-and-paper exercises which lunatics in asylums do better, and so on. But there were other interpretations: Miss Stein's own, that the opera is "a perfectly simple description of a Spanish landscape"; Julian Sawyer's, that it's a religious drama with *Parsifal* implications; and mine, dismissing Sawyer's as too academic and Miss Stein's as too modest, that it is, in a manner of speaking, the landscape itself.

As readable as it is singable, the play is to me an esthetic experience. Like a fine wine, a sunset or a wedding night, it is to be enjoyed, not defined; like a Picasso, Gris or Braque, it might be interpreted but refuses to be explained. Program notes add nothing to it, as they add nothing to a symphony.

While it was intense and dramatic, it had little to do with cognition—and I refer to the book alone in order not to cloud the issue by bestowing credit on the excellent music, conductor Alexander Smallens, artist Florine Stettheimer, choreographer Frederick Ashton and the cast and thus miss the essence of Miss Stein's own contribution, which was after all the basic motivating force. *Four Saints in Three Acts* makes no literal sense, as indeed the title foretells, for two of the five words are inaccurate; there are more than four saints and more than three acts, and no one I'm sure doubts Miss Stein's ability to count. It was intended to do something to us, not to tell us something. Of the average book it can be said that you can't take it with you, but of *Four Saints* it is on the contrary true that you can. It is not informative, like *The Making of Americans*, but it is invigorating and vastly inspiriting. Precisely like a piece of music, though in a different medium, it boils something inside you to the exploding point, serves as an intensifier, acts like sunspots on the unsteady psyche. People who resent it, and of course many were infuriated, expect too little of it; they want something they can put their finger on, and its quality is far too subtle and intangible for that.

The old joke about "why don't you say what you mean" and "why don't you mean what you say" is a reminder that Miss Stein was not the first person to suspect that words can be mankind's most dangerous invention, more catastrophic than the atomic bomb, which in fact obeys them. Like the blast of a trumpet, they can bring down the walls of Jericho. They vary much as colors vary from morning to noon to dusk to night. They are to be set in rings and bangles, or to fondle, to put your money in, to tell of love, to summon the plumber. Miss Stein, believing there was more in them, and less, than the dictionaries taught, said in *Everybody's* that she liked "anything a word can do." She showed it excitingly in *Four Saints*.

She understood words in Webster's sense, too, as we devote them to practical use, for she was expert in the traditional employment of language, as no phrase proves better than the famous, acutely stylized "A bell within me rang," to announce Miss Toklas' trio of geniuses. Starting with the familiar "that rings a bell in me," she turned it around and thus seized the advantage of association with the idiom and avoided the disadvantage of a literal copy. But in addition she had to decide on one of several possible words and orders: "A bell rang in me, a bell in me rang, a bell rang within me, within me a bell rang, in me a bell rang." One choice of words and one order alone carry the greatest emphasis and significance and best catch and hold a reader's attention, and Miss Stein hit on them unerringly. A recent misquotation of it as the "little bell which rang in my head" shows how it could be muffed. It wasn't enough for her to boast that she was a genius; she must phrase her claim in such a memorable and distinguished manner that we would not miss it nor forget its impact. The masterly form of her statement, it seems to me, verifies its content.

The woman so deft with our language understood very well what she was about, obviously, when she wrote *Four Saints*. From almost the start of her career, she knew what she wanted to do, why she wanted to do it, and how it must be done.

53

A passage from *The Making of Americans* illumines her problem and her method:

" 'I will throw the umbrella in the mud,' she [Martha Hersland, the child] was saying, and nobody heard her . . . 'I will throw the umbrella in the mud,' and there was desperate anger in her; 'I have throwed the umbrella in the mud,' burst from her, she had thrown the umbrella in the mud and no one heard her as it burst from her."

The child's emotional upsurge might represent, in the mature Stein, the impulse to act or to write; the reiteration natural to the child would be adopted as a literary method; and the author perceives that though Martha says it three times, with increasing intensity, "no one heard her."

When Miss Stein said it three times, and more, no one heard her, either. It had already happened in *Three Lives*. These novelettes, about Anna, Melanctha and Lena, where Miss Stein first introduced her repetitions, were composed while a Cézanne painting bought by her and Leo hung on the wall before her eyes. It showed the artist's wife seated in a garnet-red chair and wearing a blue dress. If the lapping of Miss Stein's dog suggested some prose rhythms to her, if common objects about her suggested words frequently employed in her writing, maybe the Cézanne, compounded of one brush stroke after another after another after another pointed the way to this novel compounded of one phrase after another after another. In the opinion of Miss Toklas, the only dependable authority, that painting exerted a considerable influence.

54

Melanctha carried on an argument in this fashion:

"About what you was just saying Dr. Campbell about living regular and all that, I certainly don't understand what you meant by what you was just saying. You ain't a bit like good people Dr. Campbell, like the good people you are always saying are just like you. I know good people Dr. Campbell, and you ain't a bit like men who are good and got religion . . ."

The ordinary concentrated to this extreme is sublimated to the extraordinary. These iterations by the Negro girl to her friend recall some Bible passages, for instance in chapter 48 of Ezekiel:

"Now these are the names of the tribes. From the north end to the coast of the way of Hethlon, as one goeth to Hamath, Hazar-Enan, the border of Damascus northward, to the coast of Hamath; for these are his sides east and west; a portion for Dan. And by the border of Dan, from the east side unto the west side, a portion for Asher. And by the border of Asher, from the east side even unto the west side, a portion for Naphtali. And by the border of Naphtali, from the east side unto the west side, a portion for Manasseh. And by the border of Manasseh, from the east side unto the west side, a portion for Ephraim. And by the border of Ephraim, from the east side even unto the west side, a portion for Reuben. And by the border of Reuben, from the east side unto the west side, a portion for Judah. And by the border of Judah, from the east side unto the west side, shall be the offering which ye shall offer of five and twenty thousand reeds in breadth, and in length as one of the other parts, from the east side unto the west side: and the sanctuary shall be in the midst of it."

A sanctuary thus buried is securely buried, but you are informed beyond question of its exact location. As a literary method this simple insistence, this backing and filling would win ridicule for Miss Stein, and high praise, and the higher praise of being imitated. Ernest Hemingway in *A Farewell to Arms* reacted to this extent:

"Lots of them would have liked him [the Duke of Aosta] to be king. He looked like a king. He was the king's uncle and commanded the third army. We were in the second army. There were some British batteries up with the third army. I had met two gunners from that lot, in Milan. They were very nice and we had a big evening. They were big and shy and embarrassed and very appreciative together of anything that happened. I wish I was with the British. It would have been much simpler. Still I would probably have been killed. Not in this ambulance business. Yes, even in the ambulance business. British ambulance drivers were killed sometimes. Well, I knew I would not be killed."

In an early letter Hemingway confessed to Miss Stein that his own work "used to be easy before I met you. I certainly was bad, gosh, I'm awfully bad now, but it's a different kind of bad."

In an article about Stieglitz, Sherwood Anderson disclosed a comparable double indebtedness both in repetition and cadence: "They have all been trying to stand up on their feet. I have been trying. I have seen others trying. It has been going on since I was a child.

"The cities try to stand on their feet. The buildings in the cities try."

These authors have turned Flaubert's rules topsy-turvy. Instead of never repeating any word on any page, they repeat repeat repeat within a sentence or line. And they have evolved a new kind of mot juste which is not linguistically but idiomatically exact. The very writers bitterly accused of rejecting the world have on the contrary marched literature right out into Main Street. This is the opposite of obscurity; this is the most obstinate and purposeful iteration, iteration till the cows come home.

Divinity school teachers used to advise aspirant pastors to say everything three times if they expected their congregations to hear once. Preacherlike, Miss Stein says it three times three times; she did it not to plague her audience but to please herself, and she would describe repetitions as "soothing." Her elementary, kindergarten but exhaustive style, or modifications of it, is to be found in scores of novels today. It is concentration, or the omission of inessentials; it is the plainest, least prettified, barest way of meaning what you say and saying what you mean. No matter how loud the laughs which greet it, it is absolute insurance of being understood . . . the umbrella is in the mud.

4

"Think of anything, of cowboys or movies, of detective stories, of anybody who goes anywhere or stays at home and is an American," Miss Stein said in her lecture,

The Gradual Making of the Making of Americans, "and you will realize that it is something strictly American to conceive a space that is filled with moving, a space of time that is filled always filled with moving and my first really effort to express this thing which is an American thing began in writing *The Making of Americans.*"

If that was her first effort in that direction, it was also about her last, for her third important work, even more likely to endure than *The Making,* involved the abandonment of this objective and the substitution for it of an entirely opposite one. If in *The Making of Americans* she had tried to tell all, she tried after a fashion to tell nothing in *Tender Buttons* and most of the rest of her writing.

Three Lives and *The Making* were immediately and practically informative; *Tender Buttons* was interpretative and evocative, perhaps even prophetic. In *Lucy Church Amiably* we find: "To put into a book what is to be read in a book, bits of information and tender feeling. How do you like your two percent bits of information and tender feeling." By this time Miss Stein scorned even that small percentage of the stuff of traditional prose.

She defined the new aim thus: "I struggled with the ridding of myself of nouns. I knew that nouns must go in poetry as they had gone in prose if anything that is everything was to go on meaning something." Some of that explanation goes on meaning nothing to me, but part of it is accurate and surprisingly revealing. It was painting, to which she came late, which helped her greatly to understand, earlier than the rest of her generation, that "nouns must go"; and if "must" sounds too strong, we nevertheless learn from her that nouns may go.

For a moment we are obliged to examine what she learned from painting. Writers commonly start their careers by studying fellow writers, and artists, fellow artists. Miss Stein is a rare, and perhaps unique, example of exterior influence; she demonstrated that creative techniques are transferable from one field to another.

In her first years in San Francisco, according to her testimony and Leo's, she saw a Millet, a J. G. Brown and one of those old, stiff, circular panoramas, oil on canvas to be sure but having little resemblance otherwise to art. If Radcliffe and Johns Hopkins, or Boston and Baltimore, offered any exhibitions to stimulate her, she did not recall them; in one place it was William James and in the other, medicine. She was an adult before, under Leo's guidance, she began to frequent galleries and museums during her summers in Europe. When she was at last ready for paintings, modern paintings were ready for her; when her eyes were opened, they were opened on the first examples of the sort of art of which she became the lifelong champion. Paris was full of old-school, nineteenth-century painters, but within a decade after the Steins moved to the rue de Fleurus, they not only owned El Greco, Daumier, Gauguin, Cézanne, Renoir, Manet and Toulouse-Lautrec, but they also were committed to the new age through extensive purchases of Picasso and Matisse.

Tristan Tzara was later to charge angrily in *tran-*

sition that Miss Stein and Miss Toklas took "infinite pains . . . to lure to their house, where their collection of canvases constituted an irresistible bait, people who might be useful to them in publishing an article in this or that review." Editors and publishers are not so gullible as he pretended; if they can't be persuaded at cocktail parties, where they at least enjoy free drinks, they can't be persuaded merely by a free look, with tea, at some one else's art collection. The visits of two editors, in fact, prove how ridiculously mistaken Tzara was. T. S. Eliot told Miss Stein on a certain November 15 that he might use some work of hers in the magazine *Criterion* but it must be her latest, and she gaily risked riling him when she produced a piece called *The Fifteenth of November*. Harold Loeb of *Broom* asked for something at least as good as *Melanctha*, so she promptly sent *Finer than Melanctha*.

The truth is simple: Miss Stein was not bribing book people, she was discovering a love for pictures, tardy perhaps but profound. When she argued that people should buy them, hang them on their walls and defend them before all comers, she was speaking out of her own valuable experience. To admire works at an exhibition was one thing, but she had not stopped there; she had taken the ultimate step of accepting personal responsibility for them, acknowledging that this was what her taste amounted to, what she liked to live with, where her money went. She had run up her flag and was ready to defend it.

The first Picasso in the Stein home was bought for a hundred and fifty francs from a gallery conducted by Clovis Sagot; it was the justly famous "Jeune Fille aux Fleurs" [Young Girl With Flowers]. Leo claimed his sister once hated it, but it remained in her possession nevertheless at the time of her death. Matisse was the other important purchase, though as if foreseeing that his talent would wear thinner than the fecund Picasso's, Miss Stein eventually divested herself of all Matisses, which went to Leo and to Michael and his wife. After them, of course, there have been very few modern School of Paris painters whose work has not hung at one time or another at Number 27. The long list included all ages, all styles and all lines of thought. Yet Miss Stein continued of course to buy Picasso. As was the custom, he presented her with the portrait for which he had asked her to sit; and for many others she paid about two hundred and fifty francs apiece. They were, if nothing more, first-rate investments, for they were later worth ten to fifty times as many dollars as she expended in francs. In after years when writing brought in no money at all, she sold a picture occasionally to meet some particular bill.

When I visited the galleries with her, she was not especially informative. There was little interpretation, but merely approval or disapproval expressed in stock phrases:

"That has something . . . I do like that . . . it is not uninteresting . . . that has nothing."

She once quoted her old friend, Madame Pierlot, who was herself an amateur: "There is nothing but landscape that can go on being right, the works of man are not worth much." Yet Miss Stein, while agreeing with the praise of the works of painters, continued to assist

61

the painters, too, asking me for instance whether I could interest a Springfield museum in this one or that one, suggesting another who might be worthy of an article in the local paper, or whose exhibition I should look up in New York, or whom she was keeping in mind to show me in Paris. She drove up and down the Ain in search of a house for Balthus; she pulled strings and argued the Petit Palais into giving Sir Francis Rose a "great big show." She would do anything to help a painter or a writer: read their manuscripts, look at their paintings, recommend them personally to publishers, editors and gallery directors in both France and America. After all the gossip about the quarreling and backbiting in and around the rue de Fleurus, it is a pleasure to record her unusual generosity, her many kindnesses, her openheartedness. She didn't stop at one good deed a day. She made innumerable friends, and if she unmade a lot of them, it was often their own fault.

In 1936 she wrote me: "Francis Rose sent me all the things he has done in Indo-China that is where he is just now, one series a very beautiful one entitled the sorrows of a painter day by day, and then a number of landscapes, he still remains my favorite among the young painters, there are others who come, two Americans, one Ferren whom you know about is over there, not a stupid man and very gifted but not very very interesting and another Benno a tall sailor who does rather refined Juan Gris and whom the gallery Simon is thinking of taking on, Picasso is interested in him, then there is a Breton named Tal Juat his real name Pierre Jacob, and his work is pretty good, but I do not know whether it is more he is the present white hope and is doing my portrait, if it gets done will send you a photo . . ."

In the same years she unearthed some pictures she was willing to give away: "There are 4 Tchelitcheff's, 4 or 5 Tonnys including a portrait of me, and 3 Genia Bermans, and a few drawings, I had to pass by all of them to find Francis Rose who is certainly the big man of that lot."

Her letters mentioned the Exposition Mondiale's contemporary show, which she served as adviser and to which she lent five Picassos; wartime trips from Bilignin to see Spanish art in Geneva and Grenoble; a provincial art show she helped to organize. She wrote the most understanding book to date about Picasso; she talked painting constantly with painters, critics, amateurs and the man in the street. For a woman who had been brought up on one Brown, one Millet and one panorama, she had traveled a great distance, a distance which for many of her contemporaries was immeasurable.

The Picasso of the first decade of this century fathered the Picasso of the fourth. Yet if Miss Stein had encountered him for the first time, in all his ripe complexity, in the 1940s, it is doubtful whether she could have accepted him. He was not so different when he was not so advanced, for he did fit into a tradition. Granting that Miss Stein's freedom from allegiance to any previous school of art may have left her more open-minded than other amateurs in that period, her recognition of his potentialities, as we view them with the advantage of a present perspective, becomes a not impossible feat, though to be sure it was almost unique. If she could discern how he might develop, she could also discern how he had developed, from Ingres and Toulouse-Lautrec among others. His first paintings were different, because they were Picasso, but not too different, because they appeared at the turn of the century. The "Jeune Fille aux Fleurs," for instance, like other canvases of about the same date, is straightforward painting; a slender nude girl seen in profile holds a bouquet, and anyone with half an eye can tell it's a slender nude girl seen in profile holding a bouquet. The bold, angular design pointed to tomorrow, but in other fundamentals Picasso was a painter rooted in the comprehensible past.

A similar elementary naturalism characterizes the works, at that time, of every single one of the persons who later left it far behind. The "Jeune Fille" was about as avant-garde as Miss Stein's *Melanctha*, or the early academic painting of Matisse, or the early writings of James Joyce such as *The Dubliners* and *The Portrait of the Artist as a Young Man*. When Miss Stein advanced from *Three Lives* to *Tender Buttons*, Picasso advanced from realism to cubism, Matisse from naturalism to color effects, Joyce from *Dubliners* and *Portrait* to *Ulysses*. But it was with Picasso that Miss Stein was most closely involved, and there are many peculiarly illuminating comparisons.

They were both foreigners living in an adopted city; Miss Stein believed, furthermore, in a certain qualitative similarity between Picasso's homeland and her own. The repetition of effort required by Picasso in the eighty sittings devoted to her portrait suggests the repetition of means in her writing. Both liked to quarrel, and they quarreled with each other, though they always made up whereas with other people Miss Stein's quarreling brought on the end of the ending of the ending . . . Their last tiff occurred in the mid-thirties when Picasso tried his painter's hand at poetry; Miss Stein disapproved, not merely because it was an indiscreet invasion of her own field but also because she believed he could not write, and it was all settled when she seized him one evening by the coat lapels, shook him, ordered him to "go home and paint a picture," and informed me that they were again "chummy."

There were resemblances even in little things, such as the fact that they worked late at night and well into the morning hours. They were neighbors, too, for from 1938 on, Miss Stein lived two minutes away, right around the corner from his Left Bank studio which is up steep stairs and right under the roof.

Miss Stein was about thirty years old when she first met Picasso; within a decade she had shelved Leo and for her devotion to her brother had substituted a somewhat comparable devotion to the painter. In the Toklas *Autobiography* Miss Stein thought the young Spaniard "remarkably beautiful" and he, according to Fernande, was impressed at first sight:

"Seduced by the physical personality of the woman, he had proposed doing her portrait even without waiting to know her better."

This mutual admiration did not exclude Fernande, however, whose relations with Miss Stein remained completely friendly. Miss Stein had praised Fernande's attractiveness ungrudgingly, and the French girl was more than fair in expressing her appreciation of Miss Stein's "ample majesty." If Leo and his sister came to Picasso's rescue when his pockets were empty, Miss Stein acted promptly by asking Miss Toklas to engage Fernande, a former teacher, for language lessons when a temporary separation from the painter menaced his mistress with hard times . . . But when they were apart, it was Pablo, not Fernande, whom Miss Stein supplied regularly with the Katzenjammer Kids and other American "funny papers" for which the artist had a passion.

On the first visit to Picasso's studio, Gertrude and Leo bought eight hundred francs' worth of pictures, a lot of money to invest in one artist in a city overflowing with them. That was followed by the many sittings, at some of which Fernande was present, in a bare room too cold for comfort in winter, too hot in summer; and Miss Stein posed in a broken chair. Yet all her life she was accustomed to comfort and invariably insisted upon it.

If Miss Stein kept one eye on a Cézanne while she wrote *The Making of Americans*—in which incidentally the town of Gossols, or Oakland, California, can be derived only from the Gosol, Spain, where Picasso and Fernande spent the summer of 1906—it seems probable that to an even greater extent she kept one eye on a Picasso, if not on Picasso, while she did *Tender Buttons*. Her writing in this period was painting, as she herself defined it. Mable Dodge is reported to have said: "Gertrude Stein is doing with words what Picasso is doing with paint." Furthermore, she was doing it in the same place, Spain, where she acknowledged that her style began to change. In 1909 Picasso brought back from his native land his, and presumably the, first three cubist paintings, two of them still in the Stein collection; and *Tender Buttons*, published in 1914, was begun in Spain. "She used words cubistically," Leo would write.

Tender Buttons is to writing, then, exactly, what cubism is to art. Both book and picture appeared in, belong to, can't be removed from, our time. That particular quality in them which is usually ridiculed, the disparate, the dispersed, the getting onto a horse and riding off in all directions, the atomization of their respective materials, the distorted vision, all that was not imagined but rather drawn out of their unique age. If the twentieth century makes sense, so do Stein and Picasso.

When Miss Stein defined *Four Saints* as a "perfectly simple description" of a Spanish scene, she must have remembered how she tantalized rue de Fleurus visitors by showing them first a Picasso cubist picture of a Spanish village and then an actual photograph, quite like the painting, of the village itself. When she wrote *Tender Buttons* in order to get rid of nouns, as she explained, she did almost literally what Picasso had done in cubism when he got rid of the objects which nouns grammatically represent.

Stray sentences from *Tender Buttons* illustrate how she demolished traditional meanings:

"The sudden spoon is the wound in the decision . . . Please a round it is a ticket . . . Oh chance to say, oh nice old pole . . . Chest not valuable, be papered . . . Why is lamb cheaper, it is cheaper because so little is more . . . Cuddling comes in continuing a change . . . Act so there is no use in a centre . . . To being the same four are no more than were taller."

A complete passage, called "Cups," may be more helpful:

"A single example of excellence is in the meat. A bent stick is surging and might all might is mental. A grand clothes is searching out a candle not that wheatly not that by more than an owl and a path. A ham is proud of cocoanut.

"A cup is neglected by being all in size. It is a handle and meadows and sugar any sugar.

"A cup is neglected by being full of size. It shows no shade, in come little wood cuts and blessing and nearly not that not with a wild bought in, not at all so polite, not nearly so behind.

"Cups crane in. They need a pet oyster, they need it so hoary and nearly choice. The best slam is utter. Nearly be freeze.

"Why is a cup a stir and a behave. Why is it so seen.

"A cup is readily shaded, it has in between no sense that is to say music, memory, musical memory.

"Peanuts blame, a half sand is holey and nearly."

These sentences resemble incoherent fragments, or nonsense, or pied type, yet they may be likened to a literal transcription of a Picasso picture, and Miss Stein inserted in one of her prose passages the admonition to "do this in painting." The artist's "Student With a Pipe," which Miss Stein owned, lends itself roughly to such treatment. Here it is, not described but restated:

68

"Pasted paper is my delight. Linotype is dot-shaped. Tent, tentacle and tentative pipe, with a waviness. Oh ear lost in behind, and warm vanilla umbrella."

To turn prose into picture, in the opposite direction, the sentence, "Act so there is no use in a centre," might inspire a work of art, and the paragraph beginning "A cup is neglected by being full of size" would make an abstract painting. In fact it is one.

A word can be exciting in itself, just as nose or ear removed from the context of face can be; perhaps if for nose and ear we substitute lips and cheek, or warm lips and soft cheek, the independent value of these isolated features becomes more understandable. Miss Stein's sentences should be read as one "reads" a painting composed of real and unreal elements, or of displaced fragments. The impressionists, whose poet was Mallarmé, separated colors into their parts, but they would unite again. The cubists separated objects into pieces which all the king's horses and all the king's men couldn't put together again. Miss Stein was equally destructive.

Her writing is harder than traditional prose, as a foreign tongue is harder than a native tongue; at first glance we catch a word here and there, or a phrase or two, but the over-all meaning must be figured out arduously. Yet a tension is created, a question asked and in Miss Stein at her best, dramatic content mounts to a climax and then a conclusion. It's pure creative activity, an exudation of personality, a discharge, and it can't be defined more exactly. The mysterious surge of energy which impels a boy who is idling on a corner to race madly down the street is part and parcel of the same thing. When people call it elementary, they mean elemental.

To this generic interpretation some persons prefer paraphrases, or literal translations, and there may be a scholarly interest in tracing some remarks to their source. "Suspect the second man" inserted in one poem derives from a robbery in Florence. The phrase in *The Mother of Us All* about turning down a lamp to get a big explosion is a souvenir of a literary rivalry between two of Miss Stein's most distinguished contemporaries. But this seems to me dry-as-dust speculation; it isn't the parts that count, but the whole. The poems and novels were not meant as puzzles.

Miss Stein's works can of course be taken literally, in somewhat the same manner in which one investigates a passage in Joyce, with dictionaries and encyclopedias at one's elbow. You dissect them, or rather vivisect them, though you're the one to be hurt and you derive little benefit from it; at the same time the magic vanishes. Either you try it on a fine example of Stein and the essence of it evades you, or you try it on an example so obvious that the effort is superfluous. Consider this subsection called "Another Play" from *Identity a Poem,* printed in *What Are Masterpieces:*

"A man coming.

"Yes there is a great deal of use in a man coming but will he come at all if he does come will he come here.

"How do you like it if he comes and looks like that. Not at all later. Well any way he does come and if he likes it he will come again.

"Later when another man comes

"He does not come.

"Girls coming. There is no use in girls coming.

"Well any way he does come and if he likes it he will come again."

A passage reminiscent of this occurs in *The Mother of Us All,* and another similar passage did not survive in the opera, for Thomson did not set it to music.

As some commentators emphasize, these words mean what they say, and Miss Stein indeed claimed to use all words in their exact sense. Yet here it seems to me that, while in the first place she ignores her conviction that nothing reveals character so little as the sexual act, in the second place she drops back to the pedestrian and the literal which her grander works surmount. What I cherish is her marvelous ability to do new things with old words, to make them lie down and roll over, sit up on their haunches, bark and often bite. "Another Play" is too easy, rather an imitation than the original Stein; the so-called four-letter words do not fit her great scale. When she defines her subject matter, she ceases to be any more interesting than the average author who is professedly concerned with nothing but "bits of information and tender feeling." Her brother Leo said of a couple of sentences, but not hers, that though he didn't know what they meant he thought they were wonderful. When Miss Stein was writing such sentences, she was inimitable.

Mankind, which used to take pride in its advance from the unknown to the known, has about-faced and now flies at breakneck speed from the known to the unknown. That is the direction followed by Stein and

Picasso, and followed by them perhaps first of us all. Our world is not only modern but modernist; and modernist painter and modernist writer, brother and sister under the skin, are so to speak imbedded in its crust, so that its shape is inevitably their shape, too. It is the world of disintegration, bursting-apart, explosion and collapse, of tremendous political, economic and ideological as well as artistic incoherence. We are the one-hoss shay.

Miss Stein's discovery of an affinity to Picasso is not surprising, therefore, since she was prepared, at least subconsciously, to pioneer in writing as he did in art; it wasn't accident but sign of the times. She benefited, or suffered, from a twentieth-century temperament. More than her physical personality induced him to paint her portrait, and more than her desire for it led her to submit to the endless sittings. The two of them groped along the same obscure trail, yearned for the same fulfillment. They were fellow travelers.

In the rue Ravignan studio and the rue de Fleurus study, the sense of anything larger than the word or the particle was demolished. Artist and writer took to pieces. They labored out of an inner conviction which could be gay but which was primarily in tune with our bleak times. Picasso defined his paintings as "a sum of destructions." And Miss Stein did not write in fragments, but instead gave us the fragmentation, the ultimate dissolution of the traditional literary form. It was atomic dissolution in the world of letters; she turned down the lamp for the sake of the big explosion.

Dissolution, destruction, atom and fission suggest

contemporary manifestations infinitely more momentous than Miss Stein's writing had ever pretended to be, or ever seemed to be either to her friends or foes. It would be as erroneous to read into her work the ultimate meaning of the modern world as to read into it nothing. Yet even if we do not claim for her the role of prophet, it is fair to point out that her devastating manipulation of words was followed by the addition to our language of a couple of very strange and awesome place names. If all the king's horses and all the king's men couldn't do anything for the nouns demolished by Miss Stein, they couldn't do anything, either, for Hiroshima and Bikini.

5

The best publicized of all the literary-artistic melees in which Miss Stein was involved followed the appearance of the Toklas *Autobiography*. In 1935 *transition* issued a fiery pamphlet, *Testimony Against Gertrude Stein*. The authors were editor Eugene Jolas, his wife Maria Jolas, Georges Braque, Henri Matisse, Tristan Tzara and André Salmon.

Madame Jolas charged indignantly that her husband's role as "director and intellectual animateur" was submerged, perhaps deliberately, in Miss Stein's account of her transactions with the magazine, and that Elliot Paul received more credit than he deserved.

Tzara, brushed off in the *Autobiography* as "a pleasant and not very exciting cousin," could have been expected to make something out of it, and he did. The memoirs, he retorted, showed "how far the limits of indecency can be pushed" and then, with an impudence which cannot be matched in the *Autobiography*, referred to Miss Toklas as Miss Stein's "secretary," his quotes, just as Salmon maliciously identified Miss Stein and Miss Toklas as "the Stein's," his quotes and also his punctuation.

"Miss Stein understood nothing of what went on around her," declared Braque, whose pique may be traced to the fact that she named Picasso and not him as the founder of cubism. Salmon swears he was not drunk at the famous Rousseau banquet, twenty years before when, in what sounds suspiciously like a defense, "we were all young" . . . though Miss Stein, familiar with fellow expatriates, had had plenty of experience in recognizing drunks; and Salmon adds, flinging up his hands, so to speak: "What incomprehension of an epoch!"

Matisse charged that Miss Stein never once mentioned Madame Michael Stein, who happened to be his, Matisse's, pupil and so, as he describes her, "the really intelligently sensitive member of the family"; refutes a couple of other details and denies specifically that Madame Matisse had a "firm large loosely hung mouth like a horse." Jolas in his foreword testifies for them all, presumably, when he asserts with multisyllabic eloquence:

"*The Autobiography of Alice B. Toklas*, in its hollow, tinsel bohemianism and egocentric deformations, may very well become one day the symbol of the decadence that hovers over contemporary literature."

74

As Miss Stein later explained with her usual perspicacity, it was the painters rather than the writers who found fault with the Toklas *Autobiography*. Writers, she said, were really curious about people, but painters, who suffered from an entirely different sort of egotism, were not. And she added further that the attack in *transition* was never published in French, the language which would have made it available, as the *Autobiography* was, to the persons most familiar with the situation and most competent to judge. Miss Stein won hands down, or so it looked from where I sat, principally because she kept her temper.

Though the fur flew, no one was shot, beaten, slapped or scratched. There were more friends than enemies, and Joyce himself, idol of the *transition* group, met Miss Stein most amicably a few years before his death. Paris being a city of innumerable little entities, each with its overlord, followers might encounter one another in rival courts but leaders, as in the case of Stein and Joyce, could spend years without meeting. A letter to me from Miss Stein says:

"And then there was a historic moment the other day that will amuse you, you know in all these years Joyce and I had never met, well the other day Jo Davidson gave a party for his Walt Whitman [sculpture] and Sylvia Beach was there and she came up to me and said Joyce is here, he wants to meet you but he cannot move around on account of his eyes will you come, so of course I did, and I said we have never met and he said no although our names are always together, and then we talked Paris and where we lived and why we lived where we lived and that was all, but I thought it would interest you . . ."

And I thought it would interest you.

$\mathcal{E}$VERY DAY THEIR
DAILY ISLAND
LIVING EVERY DAY

1

"Vous attendent gare Virieu vendredi affectueusement Stein," said a wire delivered at my Paris hotel in
the spring of 1934, and composed in a French [they
await you Virieu station Friday affectionately Stein]
that I blamed on Postes, Télégraphes et Téléphones
rather than on Miss Stein.

I looked forward to this visit with the keenest
pleasure because it meant spending several days with my
friends. Now I look back on that occasion, and others like
it, with deep nostalgia and, more practically, with gratitude for the intimate glimpses which they provide of
what Miss Stein in *Narration* called "every day their
daily island living every day."

Creative processes are, I suppose, of prime interest
to people who cherish books, and underlying such processes is the routine of the writer's life, from rising to
sleeping again. In Miss Stein's case it was a little work

and a lot of germinating. It was an unhurried, apparently idle, comfortable existence. Pictures, autos and dogs were her distraction, she once remarked; and her days in the country as well as in the city consisted of a leisurely round of walks, meals, drives, calls, play with Basket, conversations about books, paintings, household affairs. It was a sort of stewing in her own juice. She read the newspaper, gossiped with Miss Toklas, lounged in a deck chair gazing off dreamily into the distance or pulling gently at Basket's ears as he stretched out in her lap . . . and all these things were developed in her writing, out of the Bilignin sky the magpies and from the parks of Paris the pigeons alas in *Four Saints*, out of Basket the dogs in her books, and out of gossip characters.

A genius didn't need to think, in Miss Stein's opinion; he was merely a genius. "In a real master-piece there is no thought," she claimed in *Geographical History*. Her life and her works contradict these beliefs to a certain degree, but in the years of our acquaintance she could lie fallow and at the same time be extremely sociable, so that to visit her was to have a good time. You could expect her to ask if you wouldn't like to read a manuscript, scrawled in her longhand on the ruled pages of a French school child's "exercise book"; there would be serious moments but never heavy ones; and there was a lot of what New Englanders call gallivanting around to the neighbors' homes, near-by towns and sites of historic importance or natural charm. Always it was fun, and I was glad when Miss Stein's wire was followed by a letter from Miss Toklas informing me about Paris-Lyon-Méditerranée trains and continuing:

"We are having heavenly weather—it looks as if it might last so that you could see this lovely part of the country at its best—clouds in a blue sky is its specialty."

But that wasn't all: "I'm asking an enormous favor of you. Will you undertake to bring me down a largish package of linen? It would be frightfully kind of you. Indeed I'm presuming you won't mind too awfully and asking to have it sent to you at your hotel. And thanks so very much."

The linen, which arrived before the explanation, was not in one largish package but in two enormous ones; if she had proposed a largish favor and an enormous amount of linen, the adjectives would have been distributed more accurately. The hotel must have mobilized a staff of servants to cart it up to my room. When I asked the desk what it was all about, the clerk knew only that a man in a limousine had stopped at the entrance, the chauffeur had lugged the stuff in, and it was for me, he said eying me suspiciously, for me.

The letter, identifying Michael Stein as the man in the automobile, solved the mystery, though in a way I, who grouch about bringing parcels home from the corner store, was happier ignorant. A light bag would have supplied my wants for a weekend in Bilignin and I could thus dispense with porters yet not pull my arms out of their sockets. As it was, I had to have help from room to lobby, from lobby to taxi, and at the Gare de Lyon a porter with a hand truck wheeled the packages to my compartment; too big and heavy for the overhead rack, they stood out in the corridor.

Of course I was very glad to help. It is a European habit, and a sensible one, not to pay for delivery when a friendly messenger is available. Thornton Wilder, for instance, brought back a big "Exposition Mondiale" poster from Miss Stein in Paris as far as New Haven, and there thankfully found that an express company did have what he called "facilities for the transportation of white elephants" on to the Kiddies in Springfield. In the summer of 1947, Virgil Thomson in New York sent to Miss Toklas in Paris, via acquaintances who were crossing the Atlantic, whole cases of canned foods and a vacuum cleaner with all the attachments. The couple who took over the food landed in Le Havre at the time of a rail strike and had to taxi to Paris with the extra load, but would willingly do the same favor again. I never knew or heard of a man or woman who was not delighted to be of service to Miss Stein and Miss Toklas, or whom they in turn were not delighted to aid even at real inconvenience to themselves.

Callers who came for tea and talk had exercise thrown in. In World War I soldiers along the highways, with or without the reward of a lift, were asked to investigate carburetor, coil or whatever had stalled "Auntie"; when the only available coal had to be carted from distant yards in bags, a gendarme walking the rue de Fleurus beat kept them supplied, and dropped in frequently and voluntarily to do odd jobs about the apartment in his spare evenings.

It could happen in the country as well as the city, as it did to Thornton Wilder and me at Bilignin, though we both had asked for exercise; we cleared weeds from a part, a very small part it is true, of the terrace paths. Miss Stein joked about it in a letter:

"Today I began to clean the paths having finished the hedges and I began at the corner the Kiddy did because there the growth was thickest and I wondered why and I concluded that it was because he had larded the lean earth as he went along, another thing that might make a poem for Mrs. Kiddy is that just in that spot is a heavy growth of wild onions, now that symbolizes what . . ."

Despite the spinster spirit of Miss Stein and Miss Toklas, a man was handy once in a while. In the early years an American rigged up chains or strings to raise and lower the lamps in the rue de Fleurus. Braque, who was tall, used to hold paintings up to the wall to see where they belonged, and some one else hammered the nails. In 1934 while Miss Stein worked on the lectures for her American tour, she wrote:

"There is a very nice young Harvard fellow [James Laughlin of the present publishing house, New Directions] here now and he is making an abstract of the lectures to be used for newspapers, as soon as we have them all we will send them on to you, he has had his training in the *Harvard Advocate* and is doing it not so badly, he came here quite accidentally and we are making him useful . . ."

When they moved from the rue de Fleurus to rue Christine in 1937–38: "A nice English boy is offering to move my books, we accept all offers" and "it is not as bad as it might be because we make Georges Maratier do all the unpleasant work."

81

One night at Bilignin just before I turned out my light, Miss Stein tramped down the hall, rapped on the door, opened and called for help. In the darkness where her old-fashioned, long-legged underwear with trap door didn't show too clearly, I followed her to her room and Miss Toklas'; an outside blind had swung loose in the wind and I hoisted it up on its hinges again.

So as the train neared the Virieu station, where my two friends waited indeed "affectueusement," I dragged my packages, too bulky to pass out the window, to the exit. We loaded them into the Ford and started off. As we were driving through Belley, we spotted the plumber, poor fellow, and stopped.

Miss Toklas had noted in her invitation: "We are settling in slowly—you wont mind its being a bit rough —The running hot water is promised for this evening— it's a luxury rather than a habit—not a year old yet."

Afterward, when my personal experience with the running hot water proved that while it was always water and usually running, it was not invariably hot and so not always a heater, I asked about it in a letter and Miss Stein answered:

"Your question about the heating apparatus was timely, for the first time since we have had it it has been working and pray God your asking about it does not put it out, if it does we will never mention it because we will be too polite but we will hope that it will go again to bathe the Kiddies anyway it seems it was not the fault of the apparatus but of the chimney and it took us 3 years to find that out, in fact I found it out one day and we built a new chimney, but if you find out everything there is nothing to find out and how then can the time pass without your being conscious of it, after all that is the object of xistence and therefore Utopias are eventually non-xistent, because in a Utopia you would know there was no time because there would be nothing to make it pass and so there would be all the time well anyway . . ." [The phrase "well anyway" followed many of her asides, as if she was conscious of stretching a point too far; it was like an apology, an embarrassed blush, an excuse-this-please.]

They did find a good plumber once, while moving to rue Christine: "But gracious it is hard getting it [the new apartment] ready, the funny part of it the only angel of the lot was the plumber prompt efficient and obliging, so Alice does not sigh for an American plumber any more."

That was premature, for after the war Miss Toklas returned to her original complaint; of all the things she would like sent from this country to depleted France, her first choice would be a dependable American plumber. In the summer of 1947 she was still fighting with a Frenchman who was, she said, charming but charming, yet utterly unable to do anything but anything with his hands.

The luckless working man whom we stopped in the non-Utopia of Belley was given to understand that the job he had contracted to do was still not done. Miss Stein in the front seat and Miss Toklas in the rear both explained the situation. He couldn't understand, and I couldn't either, though in part that was because of the inadequacy of my plumbing vocabulary. Waving Miss

Stein quiet, Miss Toklas tackled him singlehanded. Then over her shoulder and in English, Miss Stein began to ask Miss Toklas not to be quite so severe, and Miss Toklas, hardly interrupting her tart comments, retorted that the only way to get anything done was to holler for it, and she intended to holler.

Within a couple of years Miss Stein was converted to the same practice: "We are xhausted changing an old Ford car into a new one, the old one was getting to the repairing stage and we both thought we better have a new one, and it is wearing making up your minds and then hollering to get it to-morrow and not a week hence, because whoever in France makes the most noise gets it first, so we got it to-day . . ."

2

We reached the one-street, four-or-five house community of Bilignin, too small to be a suburb of Belley as Belley is too small to possess one, so merely an outlying part of town. Beneath just the sort of beautiful sky which Miss Toklas had predicted, we turned off the main route to a short, winding dirt road, sent some chickens squawking off under the weather-beaten walls of a small farmstead, swung sharply toward the narrowest gate a Ford ever negotiated, and squeezed through without a scratch.

There we were in a yard, the spindly grass uncut, the bare, white-plaster wall of the manor house before us. It has been described already in word and picture, but it is a remarkable place, at second glance. At first, it is a typical two-and-a-half-story building, uninviting except for the entrance. Then you walk out of the bright sun through a cool, stone-flagged corridor with storeroom, stairs and dining room on the left and dark kitchen and Miss Toklas' office on the right, onto a terrace from which you look off in the general direction of the upper Rhône. The deep valley is checkered with lines and clusters of trees and neat squares of fields; hills rising majestically beyond them form a splendid prospect, with an Alpine beauty but without an overpowering Alpine grandeur.

The terrace is charming. Pebbled paths encircle box hedges and formal beds of flowers. A low wall accented by three square towers with tiled and peaked roofs guards against a drop down the hillside. Lizards race over the masonry in the hot sun. A green creeper spreads over the side of the white house.

At that time Miss Stein kept only a few paintings there, though during the war it was the refuge of her choicest treasures, principally her last Cézanne and her portrait by Picasso, rescued from Paris the minute hostilities commenced. Brillat-Savarin, gourmet, was related to the owners of the house, and some of his furniture was still used, including the bed in which I slept, I suspect unkindly, for the mattress felt as if he had stored his pots and pans in it. It was an eighteenth-century building, and by digging and scratching at the wall of my bedroom you could uncover, if you were enough of an art lover, or vandal, as were the painter Sir Francis Rose among other visitors and Miss Stein herself, the original wallpaper.

Miss Stein and Miss Toklas loved that country, which was neither an artists' colony nor a vacation resort nor a retreat for society, but plain rural France, and made their summer home there for twenty years. They discovered it by chance when, on an auto trip to Antibes to visit the Picassos, they stopped at the Belley hotel. It became their headquarters. Their suite was too cramped, they soon learned, for the painstaking job of correcting proof on *The Making of Americans*, which had been set by French printers and was full of errors. When they took their loose pages out into the fields, gusts of wind and swarms of bugs pestered them.

Out on a drive they sighted the Bilignin manor house in the distance and decided there and then to rent it if they could. They put in their bid, but the occupant stayed for three more years. One sentence in *Lucy Church Amiably* may be a description of Miss Stein waiting to enter her new home. It is a non-stop sentence which no real estate agent will ever quote in a prospectus, but I am completely sold on it. It marks time just as Miss Stein and Miss Toklas were having to do; it twiddles its thumbs. It does not state specifically that three years passed, but it reproduces the sensation of a postponement, and reflects the mounting anticipation of the two women. Other writers often adapt their own experiences, or those of neighbors or relatives, to their own literary purposes. Miss Stein, even on some occasions when she seems to be most incomprehensible, may be recreating in her style events that had occurred in her life. Well anyway, her sentence reads:

"She was not able to take possession at once as it

was at the time occupied by a lieutenant in the french navy who was not able to make other arrangements and as the owner of the house was unwilling to disturb one who in his way had been able to be devoted to the land which had given birth and pleasure to them both there inevitably was and would be delay in the enjoyment of the very pleasant situation which occupying the house so well adapted to the pleasures of agreeableness and delicacy would undoubtedly continue."

Bilignin was not far from Aix-les-Bains and Chambéry. A murder in the neighborhood had been celebrated in a novelette by Balzac, who was acquainted with one of the principals. Lamartine, who had frequented the region, ate well, Miss Stein learned somewhere, and it was a double pleasure, epicurean and literary, to follow in his hallowed footsteps.

Meals at the Stein-Toklas house were the very best in every way. Miss Stein ate sparingly, to be sure, no coffee, no wine, but meats, poultry, fish, game with their attendant delectable sauces, and vegetables cooked to perfection, and green salads. When Leo Stein boasted that he could cook and Gertrude could not, he reckoned without Miss Toklas. She knew more recipes than a professional chef, and unlike many professionals, could make them come out right. Cookbooks were and are her favorite reading and she has always wanted to write one. Americans will accept substitutes, near butter, imitation oil and the like, but the French would about as soon not eat, and Miss Toklas is French in this respect. She cooks with only fresh butter, and a lot of it; she buys coffee raw and roasts it to suit her own taste; she uses all kinds of spices, plus some kind of wizardry which makes any dish she prepares very special. For herself and guests she serves the vin du pays. When she says breakfast food, she doesn't mean the packaged variety with cartoons on the carton to tempt the young fry, but delicious, fresh brioches and croissants. The fruit dish is always piled high with ripe figs, apricots, almonds and grapes.

On a marketing trip with her I learned the difference between the excellence with which many people are content and the perfection which alone satisfies her. While Miss Stein and Mrs. Kiddie wandered off to see the Casino, the baths, the square and the flower stalls in Aix, Miss Toklas entered a butcher shop to buy a leg of lamb. The lamb must have grazed in salt meadows, and there were several to chose from. Judging by color, looks, feel, smell, weight, shape and I don't know what else, Miss Toklas finally made her selection. Then she stood over the butcher vigilantly, and refused this morsel, demanded that one, and directed every stroke of his knife, every twist of the meat, every pull of the string with which it was tied. If I had been the butcher, I would have cut her up before I was through. But once we sat down to eat, I began to have a vague idea of the interminable process, starting in distant pasturage, of preparing a faultless roast.

If we enjoyed the best food in France in the Bilignin dining room, we enjoyed the next best at some show places in the neighborhood; these outings, whether or not there were guests, gave Miss Toklas a holiday from the kitchen and Miss Stein an excuse for an auto ride, and were a welcome change for them both. We ate superbly at an open-air restaurant on the shore of the Lac d'Annécy, and in a sidewalk restaurant in Aix where the main dish was l'hombre chevalier, a rare fish from the Lac du Bourget, which lay right across the street from our table. The fish, which must be whisked out of water directly into the pot, was once flown to Paris for the delectation of a club of gourmets. On a trip to Geneva with Thornton Wilder, we had truite au bleu, or trout dropped alive in boiling water which fixes it in a beautiful and awesome blue arc.

Game abounds in the surrounding hills and forests, and Miss Stein and Miss Toklas benefited from that during the lean war years. It is excellent country for fish; a Frenchman working any of the many streams for five minutes returns with a larger catch than he could make after five weeks on the banks of the Seine in Paris.

When the lecture tour took Miss Stein and Miss Toklas to the Kiddies' in Springfield, Mrs. Kiddie served for one lunch a corn pudding made of corn raised on my mother's farm and canned by her. Since the visitors exclaimed over it, I volunteered to mail them some seed and did so from the farm the first season and afterward from a commercial seed house. That resulted in good meals for the Bilignites and good letters for the Kiddies, who were told when it was planted, how it was growing, when it was picked and how it tasted. A sizable package was shipped to their gardener in the early winter of 1935, while they were still in the United States, and was already sprouting by the time they returned to the country after long enough in Paris, as the practical Miss Toklas wrote, to clean the apartment and get it dirty again.

"The corn grows, it is sweet of it to grow and remind us of you both," was the first report, on the back of a postcard.

Unaware that corn was said not to produce satisfactory seed in European soil, I advised them to save some ears for the next planting time. Unlike the seed, the suggestion did not fall on fertile ground:

"The corn I hoed it grows but we will not keep it we will eat it. The tassles are tassling and the silky silk is shining and we are proud as can be, the lack of water dried up everything else but not the American corn, and we are tremendously looking forward to eating it soon."

At last they had sampled it: "We ate our first corn yesterday and it was delicious whether it was as good as in America we don't know but it was delicious and all due to Kiddie's mother that grew the corn that Mildred cooked and all due to the delicious way Mildred cooked the corn that Kiddy's mother grew and all due to the Kiddie who sent the corn that we have grown, anyway we are very happy with the corn."

Her letters touch upon the subject again and again. In part it was just something to fill another paragraph; or a bit of news to show how they were occupied. In part, also, she was answering my questions, for I wanted to be sure she enjoyed it enough to go to the bother of raising it, and I was checking, too, on the quality of the seed. Over the years I received seasonal reports, sometimes exhaustive, sometimes just a word in passing:

"This year we will be going down to plant it ourselves . . . It's so hot that the corn is drying up . . . The corn fills a gap [in wartime] only one has to run around a lot to find the butter to go with it . . . We are eating the corn everybody is eating the corn and everybody is as happy as happy can be with the same, even the farmers are getting a passion for American corn and the bourgeois de Belley, Mme. Roux is responsible for the Bilignin enthusiasm and Mme Chaboux for the Belley, so one of these days they will be selling tinned corn in Belley and so every war will have its use . . . Our corn has gone a little puny, but may be it was because the seed was too old, Madame Roux is in tears because she loves it . . . We saved seed and so we will be able to eat the corn of our native land . . ."

In 1937 there was a catastrophe: "The corn the lovely corn came alright to Bilignin before we got there was sent to Paris and came alright to Paris and by us was taken alright back to Bilignin and Gerald Berners [who composed the music for Miss Stein's ballet, *They Must. Be Wedded. to Their Wife.*, also called *A Wedding Bouquet*] wanted some for his garden they came to Bilignin almost immediately after we got there and it was to be sent to his gardener in England to plant and I gave Alice the Package to divide and she thought I had already divided it and so she gave the package I gave her to send to the gardener and we never spoke of it until they left and then alas for us there was none just when we were ready to plant it, but he is not a fascist [it was during the Spanish civil war, about which Miss Stein and I had argued, and I had told her I hoped none of my honest Loyalist corn would be served to any of her friends of the wrong political persuasion] no certainly not, I do not know what he is politically but I do not

91

think he does either so that is alright but we have none, could you send just a little bit so that we could plant it a little late but there might be some not much just the smallest quantity there is because it will be late."

The second World War had started when she wrote: "The day your letter came from Pennsylvania all about the corn and we were eating the last ears of our corn, the last of the season with tears in the kitchen and tears in the dining-room, because we had all loved it all summer long and we had had lots of it and every time we regaled ourselves with it we blessed the Kiddies, and Basket and Pepe have betaken themselves to the soft end of the cobs to replace bones and now even when they can get a bone they ask for a cob, such is life, and life is fascinating."

Corn was not the only food they raised, ate or wrote about. In preparation for the 1934–35 trip, Miss Stein and Miss Toklas worked up a long-distance appetite for American dishes. They expressed a curiosity about the probable fare in cities they had not visited for thirty years, so I mailed them menus from the Springfield hotel in which they were scheduled to spend two weeks. Miss Stein replied:

"We are delighted to have the menus, not only do we read them forward and backward but all the Belley-ites are passionately interested, we all do arithmetic on them all day long to find out not only what you eat and when you eat but whether it is more or less xpensive than Belley. It has been generally agreed that chickens are less xpensive in Springfield than in Belley about everything else there is a difference of opinion."

Next in importance to food, it sometimes seemed, were not literature, fame, friendship or money, but the dogs which, or maybe I should say who, frequently entered Miss Stein's books, plays and letters and filled her thoughts much of the time. I was acquainted with Pépé, hairless and pocketsize, and both Baskets, though not with the second until we were introduced at rue Christine in 1947. The first Basket, a big snow-white "royal" poodle, was demonstrative with Miss Stein but cool, or at least indifferent, to strangers. I am accustomed to dogs rushing up to eat me alive or bowl me over with affection. Nose in the air and head averted, as aloof as if he regarded himself as more than a genius, Basket did neither; he put up with people from outside the household but accustomed to quality, he refused to unbend. Pépé was Miss Toklas' dog, and often snuggled in her lap; Basket was Miss Stein's, and followed her around when she didn't follow him. Both dogs were spoiled, or both mistresses.

Pets have been cherished by other writers, celebrated or immortalized in poem and story and, like Elizabeth Barrett's Flush, they sometimes have achieved a career on the stage. Most fond owners, I suppose, have resembled Miss Stein and Miss Toklas in fussing about their dogs. The rue de Fleurus was not a ménage à deux but à quatre; there were four inhabitants, each with his daily island living, his special food, his place to sleep, even his clothes.

"I had never had any life with dogs and now I

had more life with dogs than with anyone," Miss Stein wrote in *Everybody's Autobiography*. She discovered, she claimed, a new prose rhythm in the way Basket lapped up liquids. She employed the nursery-story philosophy, "I am I because my little dog knows me," to establish abstractly her own identity, to prove that Gertrude Stein was Gertrude Stein. Dogs romped through *How to Write* and appeared on one of every four pages in *Geographical History*. There are countless references to them in Miss Stein's letters.

Baskets I and II required a great deal of care; their eyes and ears had to be cleaned, their coats kept brushed, trimmed, washed, and their nails cut, and much of this was a daily chore that fell to Miss Toklas. But the women were equally fond of the animals, and wherever they went, unless it was to cross the Channel or the Atlantic, a dog or two, like Mary's little lamb, was sure to go. The successive Baskets patronized the restaurants, sedately sitting on a bench or under the table on the floor; they paid calls; they took auto rides usually and train rides when possible. Just like humans, they were supposed to have their pride, to suffer pangs of jealousy, to demonstrate gratitude.

Basket II was the only pet left at rue Christine in 1947. Miss Toklas regularly took him out with her, though at seventy she did not need the exercise and without him could have ridden in the Métro or in a bus. She was hoping for a vacation and escape from the heat of the city, she said, but she wouldn't go without the dog. Deeply attached to her lively, playful and faithful companion, she would have endured more hardships than these for his sake. But Miss Stein would have, too, and what Miss Toklas did for Basket she did for him and for his two owners as well.

They were not admitted usually to Miss Stein's soirées because Basket was too bouncy and Pépé too apt to be stepped on. Bilignin was their favorite haunt. Pépé was too delicate for the more robust delights of the country, but Basket could run at will, dash after sticks and accompany Miss Stein on long hikes.

Both dogs were slated to come to the United States during the tour and stay with my mother on a farm, since they couldn't be kept for half a year in our city apartment. But no one in my family ever pampered a dog any more than to feed him, whistle him in at night, and make sure that he got out on time in the morning. That worried me. If one of the four-legged visitors was run over by a car or chewed up by a neighbor's animal, Miss Stein would not forgive me.

Doubts began to occur to her, too, and though the pets "would so like to see America," I read thankfully, "the more we think it over the more we think they had better stay in their native France, they might get sick from the change of climate and if anything happened at the vets they will be sad but they will know that it is only temporary, so perhaps they had better stay in France, although it breaks all our hearts."

Finally the matter was settled: "Alas the puppies are to stay here but they are to be in the care of the guardians of the Bois de Boulogne, and we hope they will be happy and will not have forgotten us."

They could get ill: "Pepe is not very happy, he

95

either feels the heat or worms, we can't do anything about the heat but we are doing the best we can about the worms, Basket is indifferent to both."

They could misbehave. Basket killed the neighbors' chickens and a little turkey; he ate "our lunch of sweet breads and reduced our chinaman to tears"; and on another day he was reported "trying to digest a stolen quarter of a cake and stolen rice pudding, it seems to be lying heavy." Miss Toklas, for whom Pépé was no troublemaker, was strict. Miss Stein left both animals free to do as they pleased; her idea of "punishing really violently" was probably to talk loud and raise her hand threateningly.

Basket provided Miss Stein with exercise which she needed. After they moved to rue Christine she discovered that she could let him loose down at the Seine by the water's edge. She also walked him around the Place St. Sulpice, about ten minutes from her apartment:

"Yes, the Hôtel Récamier [which the Kiddies once occupied] is right around the corner, that is the nice part of that part there are so many corners, I like corners [lampposts to American dogs], and just there Basket can go free because the side walks are broad and not many people on them so we are often there."

"Did we tell you," she wrote in 1936, and couldn't have been more pleased if she herself had won a Broadway success, "that Pepe is going on the stage in London in February not of course in person but by proxy, he would bark far too much in person. Lord Berners has written the music for a ballet They must be wedded to their wife, and it can't be Basket because they had a poodle in last year, to be sure it was a black poodle, but all the same so well perhaps they don't know although they act as if they do; Basket has been making up to Pepe ever since."

Miss Stein could even be confident that at a country fair the dogs would have won a prize if there had been a prize to win: "Belley is having a seventh year, that is they had one every seven years, agricultural show and we are all very xcited. Unfortunately no dogs were shown otherwise we might have had the prize, that is our dogs might have."

Then tragedy: "Basket died and it did us all up and we are just now able to smile and tell you about it."

Good news followed quickly after: "We have a baby Basket, we went to Bordeaux to get him and he is a beauty and came straight from the kennel and was scared of everything including stairways, and to-day after he vomited up the lead top of a can of Mir to polish copper which presumably he acquired in the kennel he is very happy and already so completely spoiled that he is terribly jealous of Pepe poor little Pepe who can't bite him because he has so much hair, Baby Basket has lovely eyes so we feel he is Basket's baby and we feel so much better."

Another letter began: "The poem the happy poem [one of Mrs. Kiddie's clipped from *The New Yorker*] and the happy Bone [a toy for the new dog] came for Basket II but he is being dewormed and will not be back till Friday and then the chocolate bone will taste so good after all that worm medicine and he will write you a letter to tell you so, he too has had his first proposal to

97

marriage, we are to xchange pedigrees and then when he is old enough, he is far from that yet he will be famous as a sire."

On the occasion of a bad mistake of mine in confusing Baskets I and II, I was informed that Basket II "is not shaved at all xcept his muzzle and feet, the children call him the dog in pyjamas." Wide-eyed and shrill-voiced, they still admire him as he is walked through the streets of Paris; with the permission of their mothers, who meantime discuss him with Miss Toklas, they reach out timidly to pat him; they exclaim delightedly at the "little lamb." He submits to their touch politely but like Saint Therese he is not interested. Miss Stein and Miss Toklas said that of his ABC's, he knew only his B's: Basket, bread, bone, bed and so on.

Even the roll of the seasons could be measured by the dogs. In February, 1941, for instance, "it is snowing and Basket eats it." Later: "Basket eating wood and even Pepe condescending to sniff the sun . . . Spring has come it comes more and more every minute and the radishes are showing their leaves, even Pepe condescends to take a walk, now and then . . . We were out visiting yesterday Basket and Pepe and me and we got caught in a terrible rain-storm and we all got soaked and Pepe's little coat was a sponge and we had their blankets to wash but he stepped out manfully and Alice had a fire and we dried out and that was all of that." And after a long dry spell: "But there is Pepe sneezing so perhaps the weather will change."

Strictly ornamental, they were taxed as "chiens de luxe." Basket II could and can bark deafeningly at strange steps on the rue Christine stairs, but like his predecessor and Pépé, he is really of the most complete inutility:

"We were out in the forest of St. Germain picking white hepaticas and me and the dogs got lost that is we lost Alice and the car and I finally got all the stray people in the forest looking for each other and finally with the help of an old coachman and a bicycle boy we found each other. I had told Basket to look for Alice and all he found was some deserted bread and cheese, to which he led me with great pride."

I never saw Basket do but one trick, and that was in the Bilignin bathroom. Spacious site of the running-hot-water arrangement, it was originally a bedroom and the American tenants equipped it with modern, or modern-looking, plumbing. On my first visit I was being shown the heater and other conveniences, and Basket, sniffing here and there, easily took Miss Stein's attention not only from the heater but from me. She pulled one of her large man-size handkerchiefs out of her skirt pocket and, holding a corner in each hand, waved it excitedly in the air over the dog, who began to jump for it.

"Play Hemingway," she ordered. "Be fierce."

She staged a bullfight; Basket was the ferocious animal who menaced her with death and she wagging that bit of cloth was the intrepid toreador-novelist.

The women were so fond of dogs that even toys could delight them. In March 1941 they received from us two make-believe pets, one black and one white, carved in the soap which was lacking in wartime France and named on the manufacturer's box, "Poodle and Strudle."

Miss Stein wrote with almost breathless exuberance:

"My dearest dearest beloved Kiddies:

"On the ides of March beware the Ides of March poodle and strudle did so beautifully come, I can't tell you how beautiful they are beautiful and true, I have them in my desk and I take off the cover and gaze and Alice and I try to decide whether the black is more wooly than the white or more beautifully nice, soap it is but sacred even now when soap is soap, they will never soap, bless them never never but always in their little box will they be our joy and delight, and when you come over bless you the blessed Kiddies there they will be in their lovely box unsoaping and wooly and lovely . . ."

4

During that first weekend at Bilignin we ate, talked, walked, idled on the warm terrace, paid calls and saw sights.

Parking the car in a Chambéry garage for minor repairs, we climbed a steep country road to les Charmettes where Jean-Jacques Rousseau had lived with Madame de Warens. We went to Belley and Aix to shop; drove to a mountain plateau to see an ancient church; called on friends named Giroux, d'Aiguy, Pierlot and others.

Miss Stein urged the Kiddies to come for a summer visit another year with the teasing reminder: "There is not going to be an American Queen in England but there always is us and France." The trip was arranged in 1937, at the time of the Exposition Mondiale in Paris, and when Miss Stein received definite word, she assured us, though assurance wasn't necessary, that it would be "lots of fun lots."

The French government obligingly reduced rail fares to the provinces for the tourist who first spent five days in Paris. The Kiddies traipsed around conscientiously and quite contentedly looking at new buildings, new and old art, and displays from many countries. Then just at the cut-rate deadline, they rushed off to Bilignin in response to a telegram promising, if they arrived promptly, a visit with Thornton Wilder and an auto ride to Geneva where he was to take a train.

So we left Paris, were met at the Virieu station, drove through Belley, stopped in a grocery and a cake-shop and arrived in Bilignin. Miss Toklas had cooked up a dinner and Miss Stein a party, for we were all going to attend a country dance in a small barn lighted with lanterns, with a rough floor, a fiddle or two, and a man who fired a thundering-loud pistol to announce the time to pick your partners. Inside were disheveled hair, bobbing heads, red cheeks, shuffling feet and laughter. The light spreading out through the big square door fell on a few dilapidated autos, some horse-and-buggies, and the contented faces of older onlookers. Watteau could not have painted the scene, but a Le Nain might have.

Thornton Wilder and I tried a round or two if only because Miss Stein urged it. That was what we'd come for, she said; at a dance you dance. She came, I think, because she expected we would enjoy it, and because she felt the French would be glad to have us. Her guests should mingle with her neighbors, to the pleasure of both; and while Wilder and I did our duty, she stood, her hands buried in her big pockets, balancing from one foot to the other, and watched fondly or talked with the farmers and the farmers' boys. Though I had a good time, perhaps a couple of the girls didn't.

The next day we started early for Geneva, Wilder leaving behind the terrace where he had dug weeds and done some writing and, where he had done even more writing, the Belley café which served his favorite drink, Pernod, a licorice-tasting concoction.

After farewells at the railroad station in Geneva, the four of us went sightseeing. We looked at the staid League of Nations home, at the swirling waters where Rhône and Rhine are said to start on their opposite courses, laughed again at Wilder's story about some American women saying it was pronounced Rhine and some saying Rhône, and set off along the beautiful lakeside toward Montreux and the Castle of Chillon. We explored the dingy romantic edifice which Byron helped to immortalize for visiting foreigners, viewed instruments of torture which seemed primitive compared to the devices invented in our abler generation, and peered down at the water lapping the foot of the gray walls.

Miss Stein was an admirable guide, because she let us do as we pleased. She must have visited Chillon many times, but she was not a bit impatient . . . "You sure you've seen enough . . . don't hurry, Mildred . . . did you look as long as you wanted?" She could always be counted on for the little kindnesses which matter so much.

On our return we stopped at Montreux for tea,

bought picture postcards, watched a steamer glide past, admired the swans and gaped at a lady with the first head of bright blue spangled hair we had seen. Driving back to Geneva for dinner in the restaurant where we had lunched, we had the good fortune to watch the Alpine glow turn the summit of Mont Blanc pink. After declaring to customs officers that we had nothing to declare, we left Switzerland and reached home late.

Every day there was a trip, to Chambéry again to wander through the museum, to Aix to swim, and for dinner with Raymonde Machard, who was then reputed to be the most important woman publisher in France. She had a plentiful supply of copies of her latest novel, about the glories of bearing children, and she gave the childless Kiddies a book which she inscribed: "With all sympathy."

From Aix, too, we embarked on a motor boat across the Lac du Bourget beneath the almost perpendicular face of the Dent du Chat to visit the ancient Abbaye d'Hautecombe. The House of Savoy still preserved its burial rights there, and on the abbey grounds at the water's edge we saw the old gray barn which Paul Claudel, traveler as well as poet, called the most beautiful building in the world. As usual we took more photographs and one of them, if it proves what an amateurish cameraman I am, also serves to illustrate the Stein-Toklas relationship. I thought I was focusing on Miss Stein, Miss Toklas and Mrs. Kiddie, but in the developed picture Miss Toklas was hidden completely behind Miss Stein.

The sun streaming in the window woke us early

every morning. Once we were down on the terrace, Madame Roux would bring breakfast trays loaded under Miss Toklas' supervision. About the time we were through with coffee and our second cigarettes, Miss Stein would appear in a second-floor window and in her deep voice bid us good morning, tell us the latest news in the paper, ask whether we had had enough to eat, and suggest an outing for that day. The conversation could go on for an hour.

As she stood there statuesquely, perfectly framed by the window, her forearms on the sill, with a green tracery over the white wall below her, she was as impressive as Mussolini addressing his massed followers in Rome. The Duce needed the balcony of a magnificent Renaissance façade for his setting, however, and Miss Stein achieved the same effect by speaking from the bathroom.

She had breakfasted lightly in her room, reading the mail and the Paris *Herald*, which she preferred to French papers because for one reason the ink did not rub off on Miss Toklas' sheets. She surveyed not only her guests but the new day, and a sky with cottony clouds that needed only cherubs to make it a G. B. Tiepolo scene. By this time Miss Toklas, in a wide-brimmed straw hat and with a basket hooked over one arm, was out cutting bouquets for the house or trimming the roses, clove pinks, heliotrope, sweet alyssum and mignonette.

Nights were short, for Miss Stein liked to talk and, as always, to listen. After exhausting some subjects on the terrace and more in the lighted living room, we would all go upstairs to bed, and just as the Kiddies were settling down for the night, Miss Stein would stalk into their room. There is a well known Dégas portrait of Diego Martelli seated and overflowing a little straight-backed chair. Miss Stein, on a chair against the wall beside us, her hands on her knees, motionless for long minutes and just uncomfortable enough to be alert, reminded me of Martelli. We talked about the press, which she accused of becoming impersonal; labor unions, which she feared tended to deprive the worker of his independence; John L. Lewis, for whom she evinced a considerable respect though I believe she never met him; economics, about which she was somewhat conservative; the Spanish civil war, about which she also held a very conservative point of view; government, of which she wanted as little as possible in the United States, though she seemed to favor as much of it as possible in Spain; and Franklin D. Roosevelt, of whom she did not approve. She told me:

"In America I hate to acknowledge it but in America, from the first to the second Roosevelt there has been a steady tendency to dictatorship."

She wrote half an hour a day. As she claimed in *Everybody's Autobiography*, "It takes a lot of time to be a genius, you have to sit around so much doing nothing," and in *The Making of Americans* she had already written: " I feel it and I brood over it and it comes then very simply from me." In a letter she once cautioned me: "Don't work too hard, one does a great deal more when you don't do anything, it does seem that way so if you can't go easy go as easy as you can." The Stein formula for being a genius was not of course applicable to the

Toklas job of managing the house, but that lay outside Miss Stein's domain. "What is known as work," she said, "is something that I cannot do."

Their closest friends were the family at the château of Béon: François and Robert d'Aiguy, their wives and the aged Baronne Pierlot. In the second World War the Germans would occupy the estate, clean out the wine cellars, empty all the drawers and cupboards, tether their horses in the gardens and orchards and kill the young fruit trees.

Past eighty, Madame Pierlot was as spry and active as a woman half her age. She managed the large staff of servants, the workers in the field and garden, and of course members of the family even to distant cousins of cousins. An amateur painter of talent, she was represented by a watercolor in Miss Stein's *Paris France*. Mrs. Kiddie and I own another of her little sketches, which is charming and perfectly understandable; but she wrote one hundred percent illegibly. Miss Stein, a judge of illegibility if anyone ever was, said one could never read her letters but always answered them, and I, though I could read only the "Monsieur" with which she began and then only for the obvious reason that that was the way she would be expected to begin, always answered, too. At a dinner in Paris, Anatole France once complimented her on being a provincial and told her he hoped she would stay one; but there was a worldliness about her, I felt, that was delightful. She was wrinkled, and not agile, but petite, sociable and gay.

The first time I visited her we drove from Aix along the Lac du Bourget, now down at the level of the water and again climbing a winding route cut through rock with a steep drop down to the lake on one side. A private road led to the château, which dates from the last century. I was shown some Napoleonic relics, taken to the gardens, asked to admire the view. Conversation was general, but Madame Pierlot was the principal speaker except once when Miss Stein cut loose on a topic dear to her in the midst of the depression. The trouble with the French people, she argued, was that instead of hoarding their money in their stockings as in former generations, they were spending it as if they were rich as Americans. The French must practise "avarice," she said.

At Madame Pierlot's invitation I sat beside her on a bench overlooking the fields of Culoz and the swampy land which drains into the Rhône. Once when Miss Toklas joined us, I rose to my feet to offer her my seat, in the American way. That was not the French way, and Miss Toklas declined, explaining afterward that it was impolite to surrender to anyone else the place chosen for me by our hostess. Miss Toklas is as dependable an authority on etiquette as on cooking.

If I was not informed about that French custom, neither, it developed, was Madame Pierlot informed about an American custom. After my first visit, Miss Stein sent a letter which amused her more than me:

"Madame Pierlot has the darkest designs. She wants to marry you to her cousin a lovely intellectual girl who is very excited about what she heard. They that is Mme Pierlot talks about [it] and quite nearly every time I see her, but I explain that I cannot settle the matter without you at least having seen the young lady,

107

it is not the American custom, however when you come over again she will be there . . ."

My only condition, I answered, and one which I trusted could not be met, was that the young lady should be as charming as Madame Pierlot. Miss Stein, as efficient as a marriage broker, passed that information along, and replied:

"Mme Pierlot was much pleased at your answer and she says but the young lady and myself have the same ideas, and I said but Madame Pierlot it is not ideas but charm to which my young friend referred, Ah ça, she said. The young lady was present and wanted to hear all about it all over and over again, and she will wait for you so next summer you will meet, but Mme. Pierlot was right when she said Ah ça" . . . which may be translated to mean that she wasn't sure she could deliver.

Robert d'Aiguy had a date farm in Algeria, and a commission in the army which, in prewar years, summoned him repeatedly to a post in the Maginot Line whenever the alarms sounded and the headlines blackened. François held the title of count, aspired with considerable justification to be a political seer, and contributed to the *Bugiste*, the local weekly, articles which were assembled eventually in a volume. He spent most of his time at Béon, though he and Mme. d'Aiguy had a Paris apartment. His letters were as legible as his mother's were not. Of an apoplectic complexion, merry-eyed, wearing a beret over his white hair, he was most friendly and amiable and had inherited all his mother's enviable social gifts, though the wisdom he showed early in politics petered out when he switched to the side of

Pétain and Vichy during the war. Miss Stein wrote in 1941:

"The maréchal [Pétain] came to Chambéry and Francis [François] and Rose [Robert's young daughter] and all the Légion [of World War I veterans] went to the railway crossing to protect him near Béon, but naturally they did not see him but they saw his train and that was a comfort."

Dinner at Béon, in a ground-floor room open to Alpine breezes, was a family party, a gab fest, a feast, a clutter of liveried servants at your elbow, the voice of Miss Toklas which penetrated other noises, the laughter of Miss Stein which rose above them, the shrill exclamations of François, the animated, assured dominance of Madame Pierlot. There was talk of books, crops, neighbors, America, politics. You could learn that it didn't look like a good year for grapes, or a good year for democracy . . . a gentleman from the Chambre des Députés predicted that the Chambre, too liberal for some classes in France, wouldn't last two years, and his calculation was only a year off for it vanished under Pétain in 1940.

One day they all trooped over to Miss Stein's. The Baroness, François and a couple of others arrived in an automobile ornately trimmed with shiny brass and driven by a uniformed chauffeur who wore leather puttees and elbow-length gauntlets. The guests were handed out of the car with as much ceremony as if they had come in a gilded coach-and-four, with coat of arms emblazoned on the doors. The chauffeur was Sears, Roebuck; Madame Pierlot was Queen Mary; François was Pickwickian; and the auto in a Fourth of July parade would have aroused gales of laughter. But all the ridiculous aspects were outweighed easily by the manner, the style, the graciousness, the solid-gold character of the personages. They possessed quality entirely dissociated from appearance. Even an American who scorns inherited privilege and rank would have been obliged to admit these titles seemed to fit. Exactly like Miss Stein, these people impressed you not because of what they let you see but because of what they made you feel.

After dinner we gathered around the little piano in the salon, like a band of Daumier chanteurs, and sang old French songs. Most of them were suggested by Mrs. Kiddie, who was in France to collect them for her American music publisher. We were most successful with the commoner ones, "Malbrouck s'en va-t'en guerre," "Frère Jacques," "Sur le Pont d'Avignon," "Au Clair de la Lune." Mrs. Kiddie played some accompaniments and then Madame Pierlot took over, sitting very straight, elbows tucked in, her fingers still agile on the keys but the tone they evoked dry and brittle like a music box. Miss Stein's favorite was "The Trail of the Lonesome Pine"; remembering that, we had taken her a copy from a five-and-ten. Everyone sang lustily, unself-consciously, merrily; François turned red as a beet. It wasn't musical but it was grand fun.

Miss Stein delighted in that sort of zestful party, as she had delighted in the barn dance; and every fall she and Miss Toklas attended the gay vendange at Béon, when the entire clan assembled to celebrate the vintage with an outdoor picnic dinner. Unkind acquaintances

110

have accused Miss Stein of a slight condescension toward the French; she could, they said, lord it over natives too ignorant to check on her claims to fame. But the French, who should be the best judges, have never complained. It is true that she was glad to be recognized as a celebrity, and it is true that the French were readier to appreciate her in person than the Americans who knew her mainly through her work. But to accept the homage of the French, though it might be conceit, was not condescension.

She really liked them, whether Madame Pierlot, the servants, the doctor and his wife, the farmer, the priest, or literary and artistic people in Paris. From a journalistic point of view, she had reported on them admirably; *Wars I Have Seen* contains some fascinating stories.

The only thing she did, to my knowledge, to which her French friends could have objected morally and maybe legally was to seem often to be about to run them down with her car. Though possessed with lightning-fast reactions and a knowledge of how to handle a Ford, she felt she owned the road. She spent a good deal of time driving for visits, on errands, or just for the pleasure of being at the wheel. But she regarded a corner as something to cut, and another car as something to pass, and she could scare the daylights out of all concerned.

One fine morning when she was taking Miss Toklas and the Kiddies to Aix, we raced up a steep hill toward the tunnel which pierces the mountain above the Lac du Bourget. Trying to maintain speed, we whisked around a curve and at the same moment around another slower car, and found ourselves headed straight at a third auto

111

coasting downhill at a fast clip. Miss Stein jammed on the brakes in the nick of time, and threw Miss Toklas forward so hard that she banged her head. While the other driver burst into screeching invective, we scooted off, abashed but safe.

$\mathcal{W}$E KNEW IT WAS
WONDERFUL
EVERY MINUTE IT
WAS BEING WONDERFUL

1

WHEN MY FIRST weekend at Bilignin ended on a Tuesday, I prepared regretfully to leave on the afternoon train which would arrive in Paris before midnight. After asking Miss Toklas' advice, and following it, on the proper size of tips for Madame Roux and Trac, the Annamite servant, I jumped into the car and glanced anxiously at my watch as we started for Virieu with not a minute to spare.

Hardly a hundred feet from the house, a tire went flat. I changed it at top speed, we drove on and swung in to the station. The train had gone.

Since the next one was not due for two hours, we parked and for the first time Miss Stein introduced the subject of an American lecture tour. Maybe other topics were exhausted, or maybe she suspected Fate had caused the puncture and arranged this opportunity. Carl Van Vechten had already urged a visit to her native land and there, in the shade of a tree between trains, she said later, she was definitely persuaded.

None of several formal propositions was completely satisfactory to her or especially to Miss Toklas, who has a good head for business. One proposal of a general over-all payment regardless of the number of lectures had already been rejected, and another, on a percentage basis, was still under consideration.

Miss Stein asked me as many questions as she had at Nîmes. What did America think of her as a person and as a writer? What would America think of her as a lecturer? How would the press react? Would she draw audiences? Did few readers mean few listeners? Would six lectures offer enough variety?

Though a newspaper was paying me a wage on the assumption that I knew what was news and what wasn't, I felt little confidence in my judgment in this affair, and the very nature of Miss Stein's queries betrayed the number of intangibles which would make a positive reply difficult, or at least unreliable. Did my firm conviction that Miss Stein was newsworthy merely reflect my prejudice in her behalf? If back home I offered a story about her to the city editor, would he snarl his disapproval, or snarl his approval?

The answer could not be evaded or postponed. It was my guess, I said, that she would achieve a great popular success; newspapers would be friendly, or at least curious, which from one point of view amounted to the same thing; she would have no trouble filling as many

114

dates as her strength permitted, and the halls would be crowded.

The train came at last, we bade one another farewell until fall, and I left. The very agreeable memories I had expected to bear away were overshadowed by one Grade-A worry. In my mind's eye I saw Miss Stein squeezed insultingly into half-inch fillers at the bottom of all the back pages. I was afraid I should have kept my mouth shut. From news editors she could expect the same ignominious mishandling to which she had been submitted by some critics . . . I still had to learn that no city desk reads its critics and that if it did it would not accept their judgments. Yet if Miss Stein had no press, she could not possibly have an audience.

A man's worries, even major worries like mine, were supposed to vanish before Paris' attractions, which Miss Stein had enhanced with some helpful addresses and letters of introduction. I kept busy in the galleries that exhibited Rose, Balthus, Ferren and others then little known in this country; I called on William Cook, the taximan who taught Miss Stein to drive, an American-born artist and, for my interests at that period, important largely as the occupant of a house built by Le Corbusier, and I visited Michael Stein. He too lived in a Le Corbusier house with a beautiful view of St. Cloud and the roofs and towers of Paris, and his walls were covered with paintings by Matisse. He was important in his own right, however; with little of the assertive spirit that characterized his famous sister and brother Leo, he seemed to love the arts more because he needed them than because he imagined they had any need of him.

But after a short stop in London and return to the States, where Miss Stein welcomed me with a letter: "Have a good trip, that is have had a good trip," my problem could not be evaded any longer. Fully informed about Miss Stein's current plans for the lecture tour, I was first requested to communicate with her agent in New York and discuss it with him. From then on, correspondence was devoted to this one topic:

"There have been so many alarms and excursions concerning the lecture's. X's proposition of a lecture bureau, disguised a little but still there, I had definitely refused before and have continued to refuse and we go on with what we talked about when you were here and had so pleasantly missed your train. Bernard Faÿ has suggested to me a young man Marvin Ross to do the clerical work and arrange the dates. He lives in Moriches, Long Island. As you do know very well what I want and how I want it, I would like it if you could that you would get into communication with him and help it all along. It would be most awfully nice. I am solemnly going on writing the lectures. I have finished one about pictures, one about the theatre, and am now doing the one about English literature. Then there are three about my work, Making of Americans, 2 Portraits and so-called repetition and what is and what is not, 3 Grammar and tenses. I get quite a bit of stage fright while doing them but if one must one must . . ."

This continued in the next letter: "Do write again to Marvin Ross, I have split with X he is not acting for me any more, we could not see eye to eye in this matter, I to I if you like but anyway, he is not acting as my agent any more, and I hope everything will go as we planned and Marvin Ross is acting for me. I am writing now on my fifth lecture, I tried the English literature one on a private [group] that is to say on friends here last night and I guess its pretty good. Otherwise calm, Trac has left us . . . we have gotten two other Chinamen, one of them an xstudent is like an xstudent but the other one can cook, so all is well."

In August she wrote: "Bernard Faÿ is here and we talk lectures and plans all day long and things are getting quite nicely decided, and he likes your photos and so do we and so does Trac who is not unlikely coming back, and Faÿ suggests that you tell Ross that you have taken these photos and that he may use them, Faÿ thinks he will have need of quite a number. You have a weakness for taking two at a time [on one film] but that I suppose is both New England efficiency and economy, but we are really pleased with them. Faÿ is always beginning to have Ross make preliminary announcements of the lectures in the newspapers so do whatever you think is right about that, you have the list of subjects and five of them now are all written and I do think they are pretty good and so does Faÿ."

If Miss Stein's head was in the clouds, her feet were on the ground, and she kept tabs on all the constantly changing arrangements. In letters she switched from lecture to tour and back again; the lectures will be good, she guarantees . . . she's doing her part; and how will the tour be, she asks . . . am I doing mine? If she had ordered me to do thus and so, I'm sure I would have obeyed, but she was considerate in every way, generously

117

praising the few little services I was able to perform, and offering her own, or Miss Toklas', suggestions tentatively and even apologetically:

"The only thing Faÿ thought should be done sooner was an announcement that Ross had charge of my lecturing engagements . . . but perhaps everybody does know by this time that Ross is doing it but Faÿ thinks and I am not sure that he is not right that some newspaper statement should be made at once to that effect. The publicity as you rightly say should not begin until much later and we all find all your plans concerning that xcellent and you and Ross seem to be working awfully well together. You know by this time that Random House is bringing out a book of portraits to be out the first of November and they [Random House] will do the lectures in the early spring. I am awfully happy about the book of portraits, one of the lectures that I like the best is about portraits and repetition and so the book comes just right . . . These abstracts [of the lectures] you would use as the basis of some articles and they would probably help a lot. As I say we all think that your plans are good plans and are looking forward to more. You must remember too about the traveling business that it is always xpensive for two people that have to be considered and that also we have to be reasonably comfortable if I am not to get too tired. But I am certain you and Ross between you will arrange the matter the way it should go . . . The lectures are good I have just been reading them to Faÿ and the Harvard boy [Laughlin] but they are for a pretty intelligent audience and though they are clear very clear they are not

118

too easy. I am writing this lying down because Alice and I have been working terrifically getting the mss. together for the portrait book . . ."

Ross and I discussed the situation at the home of a friend, Walter Hovey of the art library of the University of Pittsburgh. Ross's real interest was art, and he did the job while waiting for something more in his line. My real interest being Miss Stein, I emphasized her fixed habits, her custom of doing as she pleased, and her right to exactly the kind of tour she wanted. My efforts were all the greater because my rash prognostication was fresh in my memory; the tour must succeed not only for Miss Stein's sake but for mine.

At last the time drew near: "Here we are [in Paris] and then there is only one step further and there we will be there over there, we are in all probability taking the Champlain leaving here the 17 [October, 1934] and getting there so they say the 24."

A final note written aboard ship was received actually after I met them: "I was awfully scared just at the last but now we are comfortable very comfortable and very peaceful, and lots of love and always Gtde Stein."

One question of utmost importance to Miss Stein, Miss Toklas and their well-wishers: Would there be an audience, had already received a very encouraging answer, for the schedule was filling rapidly. The first lecture was to be in New York City's Colony Club on November 1, within a week of arrival. Distant places showed a considerable desire to see and hear the expatriate, and in Springfield, not including near-by engagements, there were to be an opening talk before the Century Club, a second in the Springfield Museum, and others under the auspices of University Extension.

The prime problem remained the matter of shipboard interviews. While museum directors, college presidents, professors, writers and artists stood ready to welcome the lady kindly, the reaction of the press was yet to be revealed, and no celebrity is a celebrity without pictures and stories in the papers. A thing can be news in New York and not in Boston, news on a Monday and not on a Tuesday, news to editor A and not to B, and it can't be news anywhere or at any time if something else crowds it out. But aside from all these unpredictable relative values, several possible phases of the coming encounter could be foreseen. Would she be too frightened to do justice to herself? Would her really extraordinary personality come through? Would she give proof of what Louis Bromfield believed was "the clearest intelligence I have ever encountered"? If she were in top form, would the press be too prejudiced by her prose style to appreciate her? If she were not in top form, would she rate some space nevertheless as a curiosity? Nobody likes to make page one by biting a dog, yet there is an advantage in being on page one.

My managing editor wouldn't bet one way or the other on the metropolitan press. I wouldn't, either.

Eager to be present when the issue was settled, I arranged to sail down the bay on the government cutter and meet the *Champlain* with the regular ships reporters. I was not to cover the arrival but to be the first to greet Miss Stein and Miss Toklas and judge the nature of their reception with my own eyes. After working until midnight on my paper and reaching New York sleepless five hours later, I went to the Battery, bleary-eyed but excited, and met my guide, who was to handle the Stein story for The Associated Press. He provided me with a pass and instructed me to tell the cutter commander that I intended to interview Abbé Ernest Dimnet, the popular essayist, since sightseeing, joyriding and more than one reporter from one paper to one personage were forbidden.

No questions were asked as we pulled away about dawn. When we came alongside the liner, I walked around the cutter deck to have a look and there they were, Miss Stein and Miss Toklas, way above me, peering over the rail, and we were waving frantically to one another.

2

The interview was decidedly with Miss Stein; Abbé Dimnet had picked the wrong ship and received scant attention. The main encounter, match or bout, took place in a lounge, with ten or fifteen men and a couple of women, notebooks open and pencils aimed, confronting Miss Stein. I sat behind her and Miss Toklas stood on the edge of the crowd and grinned her delight.

It would have been easier to sneak past customs with diamonds on all fingers and toes than past those alert newspapermen, who had come loaded for bear, as one of them confessed in his story. Sitting in chairs or on table tops, or squatting on the floor, they formed a ring around her. Though newsmen, unlike professors, rarely bone up before they start a job, if only because they have no time, several had copied out some of Miss Stein's more perplexing sentences so that they could challenge her explicitly and make her put up or shut up.

Before it was over, she put up and they shut up. "Why don't you write the way you talk?" they demanded, and she retorted: "Why don't you read the way I write?" There wasn't a sign of stage fright, a second of hesitation, a slightest hint of confusion. She had met the enemy and he was hers.

She had returned to this country to "tell very plainly and simply and directly, as is my fashion, what literature is." That incited them to questions as to how plain, simple and direct were *As a Wife Has a Cow a Love Story* and certain passages from *The Making of Americans* and *Four Saints*.

"You see and you hear and you have got to know the difference," she lectured them. "It's very difficult to know how much you hear when you see and see when you hear. The business of writing is to find the balance in your own inside."

Since that didn't satisfy them, she continued: "People get sot in their ways. [Every reporter instantly wrote s-o-t, sot, and followed it with a "sic".] Think of how you talk when you are not writing. You reporters don't talk as you write. As for the repetition in my writing, you repeat a great deal, but in repeating change the words just enough."

She avoided politics with the claim that her business was writing, and slyly left her questioners uncertain whether she had confused Franklin D. Roosevelt with Theodore Roosevelt, and whether she knew Coolidge had died. She described the crossing as fine, identified Miss Toklas as her secretary and the one who "makes life comfortable for me," reaffirmed her affection for Ernest Hemingway, said that Shakespeare, Trollope and Flaubert had influenced her and that she herself could not understand why she had waited thirty-one years to revisit her native land.

She posed for photographers, broadcast over a ship-to-shore radio hookup, and had her passport checked. At the foot of the gangplank, publisher Bennett Cerf and Carl Van Vechten, a friend since 1913, welcomed her, and the five of us drove to the Algonquin. By the time the two travelers were comfortably settled and had finished another long interview for a morning paper, they were ready to rest, and I was, too, so I started for the Grand Central and a train to Springfield.

Even if I had been too sleepy to glance at the newsstand in the lobby, the headlines would have shrieked up at me. There were Miss Stein and Miss Toklas on every single front page. I grabbed one armful to send back upstairs and a second to read going home. I was no longer sleepy.

3

At last the riddle was solved. The give and take aboard ship had been sharp and entertaining, and not only Miss Stein but also the reporters had had the time of their lives. The artist's "business is to be exciting," she would write in *Narration*, and she was an extraordinarily exciting person that morning. She had stood up to a steady fire of questions, and answered them without any fumbling and with the sort of forthrightness which newsmen admire and respect. Her meaning sometimes escaped them, but they obviously enjoyed the experience, as she did, and they liked her.

None of this proved, of course, that the resulting stories would pass the strict tests of jaded copy desks. But for once, sprightly interview was transformed into excellent copy. The *Sun, Post, World-Telegram* and Brooklyn *Eagle* all began their stories on page one. The *Sun* carried a two-column cut of Miss Stein and a single of Miss Toklas, and the *World-Telegram* a four-column spread showing three different views of Miss Stein's happy, smiling face. Next morning the *Times* and *Herald Tribune* printed long accounts, and the *Sun* continued with a piece in John McClain's "On the Sun Deck." Twelve columns of space were devoted to her in New York City alone within twenty-four hours of her arrival. There and then she was promoted from curiosity to celebrity.

First glance at the headlines disturbed me, for they were written not in the spirit of the following stories but, oddly, out of the general public's misconception and misconstruction of Miss Stein's work. Such headlines, by people who knew her only by hearsay, could have been composed before the deskman read the articles and must have been composed without any intelligent reading of them at all. They violated the facts of the shipboard interview. I suppose the men who dashed them off wanted to prove that, as is said jeeringly of abstract and cubist paintings, any child can do them; and they intended at the same time to disavow any serious editorial commitment to her kind of stuff. They wrote:

> "Gerty Gerty Stein Stein
> Is Back Home Home Back"

> "Gertrude Stein Barges In
> With a Stein Song to Stein"

> "Gertrude Stein, Stein
> Is Back, Back, and It's
> Still All Black, Black"

Set in thirty-six or forty-eight point bold type, they were not very funny, though they were imitated in many of the cities Miss Stein visited. But the stories, on the contrary, were accurate transcripts of the interview, and testified gratifyingly to a genuine interest in the expatriate. As one newsman admitted:

"Miss Toklas was afraid, she said, that the reporters would frighten Miss Stein, but after a few minutes Miss Stein had the reporters frightened."

There were some inaccuracies. She was not of course a "literary dictator." She could not be identified legitimately as the "Sibyl of Montparnasse," which appeared in a paper with a circulation outside of New York, evidently, since the stilted phrase, so unlike anything which Miss Stein herself might write, was picked up in other communities. Basket and Pépé would have barked and bitten the pants off the insulting newsmen who referred to them as cats.

The descriptions of what Miss Stein wore, by the

male band of reporters, were sometimes more extreme than the clothes themselves. While the men were troubled by this phase of their duty, not a one of them shirked. Her hat was called variously a braumeister's cap, a jockey's cap, a deerstalker's cap and a grouse-hunter's cap. It was a small gray tweed, it was mannish, its brim turned down "visor-like so that it gave a squirrel-like appearance to her face." One observer explained:

"A strange article, apparently a compromise between feminine toque and male cap; black and white tweed, with visor in front and coy upcurl at rear."

Another, adhering to an academic tradition which the "Sibyl of Montparnasse" had tried for forty years to eradicate, injected the highfalutin literary note into his section on millinery: "A Stein hat, a hat as persistent as the repetitions which are a feature of her abstruse writings . . . Peaked in front . . . it roamed backward tightly . . . to a fold at the rear; a gay hat which gave her the appearance of having just sprung from Robin Hood's forest."

The strange case of Miss Stein's headgear is amusing, I find in the end. She was quizzed about her writing because it was new, but once curiosity was aroused it couldn't be satisfied and it ceased to be discriminating, for the hat which attracted so much attention was old. It was especially modeled for Miss Stein after a Louis XIII, that is, thirteenth-century, hat which Miss Toklas saw and liked in the Cluny Museum. In answer to a question, Miss Stein said:

"It's just a hat."

Flights of fancy about the rest of her clothing

were more restrained. Everyone agreed on "a man's style topcoat of homespun . . . straight short skirt" or called it a "brown tweed suit tailored on the severe lines which were popular when she left America thirty years ago." It was thick cloth, with brown velvet along the edges. She had on "a cerise vest of voluminous proportions," or as it was described by a reporter who presumably consulted Miss Toklas, a "red Moroccan wool jacket." On her feet were "big men's shoes," broad, low-heeled, round-toed, "of the sensible type." Her stockings were "thick" and "woolly."

She had "merry," "remarkable," "candid brown" or "keen brown eyes," and one reporter explained that they were the "weary but penetrating eyes of an aged statesman." Her hair was iron gray, close-cropped or close-clipped, in short, "a masculine haircut." She had a "thick body," she was "stocky," she was "plump," she was "short, very sturdy," and her legs were "sturdy."

"Strong-voiced and mellow-toned," with "a constant chuckle in her throat," "laughing heartily," she had a "large nose and solid cheeks" and, added a newsman bent on cataloguing every single trait, "large ears."

"This renowned authoress," "literary eccentric," "matron saint of art in Paris," "grand old expatriate" and "enfant terrible of literature" was pictured variously as a "hearty, irreverent old lady . . . warm, alert, rugged," "an impressive figure," possessed of an "amazing and charming vitality" and "altogether charming, and as transparent as a bartender's laugh."

She "has been exceedingly sensitive to the critical guffaws directed at her work," one reporter asserted, but another evened up the score by stating that she was "not one whit disturbed by the criticisms she has received."

Yet while some of them still balked at her writing, they all extended to her a hearty welcome as a person and conversationalist. "Very understandable," "with a vivid, lucid style," they remarked, and discovered that she "spoke a language everyone could understand." One man complained that it was not easy to give an account of her, "not because her speech is difficult, or abstruse, or symbolic—for it is none of these things—but because of its actual simplicity."

"No one enjoyed that interview more than Miss Stein, unless it might have been Miss Toklas," in the opinion of one reporter, but others reacted differently to the "constant companion," "secretary and companion," "somewhat submerged heroine of *The Autobiography*," Miss Stein's "Girl Friday" and "enigmatic bodyguard and typist."

Miss Toklas' "Cossack-type" cap and black fur coat "gave her a less unusual appearance than her companion's," it was conceded. "Tiny, thin-faced, mouse-like . . . sitting quietly in a corner . . . watching, listening, grinning occasionally," she "hovered in the background." She was "rather nervous," said another paper, and then clinched the point by calling her "thin, dark, nervous-appearing." She was "worried but gracious," "dark and small," she "gazed raptly at Miss Stein." She "shrank" in the background. She was Miss Stein's "queer, birdlike shadow" and when she could be persuaded to speak at all, she "twittered."

She may have cawed and on that memorable day she

would have had a right to crow, but she never in her life "twittered." Defined by Cecil Beaton, who photographed the pair of them, as half of the team, Miss Toklas did not receive such accurate or extensive coverage as Miss Stein, yet I am certain that was the way she wanted it.

4

Miss Stein's celebrity did not depend upon the purchase of a newspaper; New Yorkers passing newsstands could discover at a glance who was visiting their town. Bennett Cerf told Miss Toklas that you "two naive ladies coming from provincial Paris teach New York what publicity is," and he had a point though his "naive" and "provincial" might be challenged.

"Everything is going famously, we continue to love N.Y.," Miss Toklas wrote before the week was out.

There were moments of doubt, however. Once in response to my congratulations on the lectures, which I had just read in their final form, Miss Stein said my letter was delivered "just the moment when I was a little low in my mind and a bit scared," for she still had not met the test of the first American audience. As the time for that approached, I received this word:

"Our xciting and most pleasant life. Oh everybody is so kind . . . your telegram before the first lecture because I did have stage fright was a comfort, but now I hope stage fright is over and everything is cheerful."

According to another letter, "Have we had a hectic time it is unbelievable, you know I did a news reel for the

Pathe people, I think it goes on to-day, and everybody knows us on the street, and they are all so sweet and kind it is unimaginable and you go into a store anywhere to buy anything and they say how do you do Miss Stein and Alice goes anywhere they say how do you do Miss Toklas and they so pleasantly speak to us on the street, its unbelievable, to-day and that was funny one man said to the woman who was with him, there goes your friend Gertrude Stein as if he had had enough and more than enough. I too thought I might be news but not like that. And we are flying to Chicago the 7 [of November] for the opera [*Four Saints*], the Curtis Air people are giving us free transportation aller et retour [round trip] which is well its all mad but most pleasurable. This afternoon, we took off, saw nobody xcept the reporter from the American, and we just sat around with everything disconnected and it was necessary . . . and good-night, and after doing nothing all afternoon we are going to bed which is again very necessary."

Excitement never flagged. There was going to be a broadcast "at the National Broadcasting" . . . and whenever she specified hours and places for speeches and the like her handwriting was legible. In Chicago: "Here we are and it is wonderful and we are very happy." And later: "We have a wonderful time, the opera was wonderful everything was wonderful." A letter from Miss Toklas continued the same refrain after they returned to New York:

"Everything has been wonderful, we are making plans for a leisurely tour of the whole country, by air of course . . . I want to stay in U.S.A. for ever. And I'm not discovering it, it's always been like that only now it's more so."

After two lectures in Cambridge, which Miss Stein "enjoyed a lot," they went back to New York again for "the Dutch Treat lunch, that was very very interesting, I liked that audience immensely and then a lecture in the evening. We are looking forward to a quiet time in Chicago, and then I am enormously looking forward to New England in January, New England is beautiful, it is very beautiful the color and light even finer than I xpected it to be . . . I cannot tell you how we have enjoyed everything."

In response to her admission that she was tired, I hoped she wouldn't catch cold, and she replied:

"As usual you are right in your warning, and I have caught a little cold but we are curing it nicely and it is practically all well,.today being Sunday I am making it a really truly day of rest, reading a shilling shocker staying in bed and writing to my friends."

Then they headed west: "We will so very soon be leaving this our dear New York. It's been wonderful really and truly wonderful and we have had a wonderful time."

Following the Chicago engagements they planned to move around until Christmas and "then we rest and get the lectures together to be printed and then we see you in Springfield and all that will be wonderfully nice and here I think we will get rested, Chicago is not going to be as beguiling as was New York which is just as well because we need a rest, those few weeks in New York were wonderful and we loved every minute of it."

They now embarked on the trip which, besides a return to New York and New England, would carry them to the Universities of Wisconsin, Iowa and Ohio, and to college and club audiences in Richmond, Charlottesville, New Orleans, St. Louis, Cleveland, St. Paul, Detroit, Ann Arbor, Indianapolis, Toledo, Washington, Baltimore, Columbus, Houston, San Francisco, Pittsburgh and many other places. Miss Stein enjoyed Virginia, but not "like I do Massachusetts and Connecticut . . . I like it all but you have to like something better than other things even so."

Miss Toklas sent a roundup of news from St. Louis: "The south was interesting and sometimes most awfully attaching. It started with Charlottesville, which was perhaps the most endearing, university, students, town and country. We quite lost our heart to it . . . Richmond was amusing, the confederacy and Mr. Lee are as present and familiar as a newsreel, but G. revenged herself by insisting upon being shown the site of Libbey prison. Chapel Hill, then Charleston, which I would have adored if G. had not caught a most frightful cold when we spent a day on a plantation and were rowed for hours upon a swamp turned lake with hanging gardens in a torrential downpour. Then New Orleans, which is more varied and amusing than S. Francisco (alas that it should be so) and which we left yesterday by air and only made Memphis because of a storm. And now we go to Chicago to-morrow where G. rests before her class [in composition] at the university."

There Miss Stein met Thornton Wilder, autographed innumerable books, attended the opera frequently, rode in a police car, and hired a drive-yourself auto.

"My Chicago course is over and we are wandering on, we like our Chicago days and we like wandering on that is the way we are now and we seem to like it, if you live in America you do wander on, and I have a drive yourself car, the tires go flat but we drive and we drove it 175 miles the other day and did not sail on an ice boat which was just as well as the ice boat went under the water . . ."

They flew in a three-seater plane from Madison to St. Paul:

"Just we two and the pilot, and over the snow hills and then the snow prairie it was unbelievably beautiful, and the symmetry of the roads and farms and turns, make something that fills me with a lot [that's what the letter says, and presumably her thoughts were flying far ahead of her pen], and the shadows of the trees on the wooded hills, well the more I see the more I do see what I like, I cannot tell you how much we like it, last night my eyes were all full of it."

From Columbus: "We have been so many places and we pretty well have liked them all and they all are so different that they come very near not being the same at all, and the lectures go awfully well and it is so wonderful to see all the places we have always known and never seen and now we want to see a lot more of them until we have seen them all. I have been enormously interested in how different one state is from another, and why, and I don't know, I am tremendously moved by the simple facts and differences here and everywhere, we have been in Michigan and Indianapolis and illinois and now Ohio, and we want to see all the others, and flying helps and we like flying, and everything helps and we like everything."

She had known Pittsburgh, San Francisco, Baltimore and Boston when she sailed for Europe thirty-one years before, and by this time she did not remember much of them, or much that fitted into this new perspective. The rapid unfolding of vast stretches of her native land would result two years later in another book, in which she developed the reflections sketched cursorily in this letter: *The Geographical History of America or the Relation of Human Nature to the Human Mind.*

Miss Stein achieved a phenomenal success and happily she was fully aware of it. "Wonderful, wonderful, wonderful" was the constant refrain of her letters, and that was purely emotional repetition, not for literary effect. Her experience forced from her one deep, coast-to-coast gasp of delight. The fondest dreams of the "tormented" years when she couldn't sell a page of manuscript fell far short of this glorious reality. From New York she wrote:

"I cannot say that we don't like it we do like it wonderfully every minute and everything has worked out so beautifully as we planned when you so providentially did not catch your train and everything is so nice . . . I am delighted really delighted with the way all the audiences take the lectures and it makes me happier than I can say . . . I went to see [Alfred] Stieglitz and he was charming, I told you what he said, he said to me I know what it is it is just a Christmas tree for you all the time, which it is . . ."

134

Matisse told her once that the world was a theatre for her; so now it was her oyster. It was also Miss Toklas': "Greetings for the merriest Xmas ever," she wrote, and she too added: "Which it is."

After a visit to the White House where they were abashed at the informality with which cabinet officers, looking as the two guests said like plumbers and laborers, hustled in and out of the reception room, they reached Springfield for a two weeks' stay at the start of the new year.

5

More than a month had passed since we had seen Miss Stein and Miss Toklas at the Brooklyn Museum. There Miss Stein made the acquaintance of Marianne Moore, and there a dignitary, ceremoniously bowing the distinguished visitors into a taxi, slammed the door shut with a flourish worthy of his position and gave Miss Stein's finger a fearful pinch, so that we had to stop at a drugstore for salve and bandage.

In Springfield Miss Stein looked tired. Chicago in prospect may not have seemed as beguiling as New York, but it proved exciting and wearing, though thanks in large part to Thornton Wilder, very pleasant, too. Christmas had not provided the anticipated rest, and Miss Stein needed to relax.

Months before, as Miss Stein looked forward to the Springfield visit, she had hoped it would be possible to take some drives through the Connecticut valley and into the Berkshires. Since we had no car, friends rallied in the most generous way to our help; they lent their autos whether or not they could come too, and one of them even lent a horse.

The arrival in my home town was without fanfare, as the visitors wanted it, but was not auspicious. The first of our friends, and a competent driver, who volunteered to meet the train and provide transportation to the hotel, bundled Miss Stein solicitously into the car and pulled away from the curb right in front of a passing machine, jammed on the brakes and forced the guest to grab for leather. Miss Stein at the wheel might have done the same thing, but like the rest of us she would rather have done it for herself. At the hotel, photographers insisted on pictures and there was endless posing, holding a book, not holding a book, full face, profile, or just immobile in front of an ornate fireplace with no fire, and looking as if she'd rather be anywhere else in the world. By then she and Miss Toklas were ready to retire to their rooms and stay by themselves until the hour of their first lecture that evening, a dress affair of the Century Club in a private residence.

There Miss Stein talked on *The Gradual Making of the Making of Americans*. Perhaps the most curious of all her western Massachusetts audiences to see and hear her, this one despite a doubting Thomas or two, responded with genuine applause. Miss Stein and Miss Toklas declined with thanks an invitation to a post-lecture supper and returned to the hotel.

Critics who rail at Miss Stein's appetite for publicity must be reminded that she would not swallow all kinds of it. People wanted to talk to her, and she would not be bothered; wanted to wine and dine her and she

136

would have few of their dinners and none of their wine. Spread the most delectable tea before her, and she would ask for a glass of Vichy water, the one thing her embarrassed hostess was certain not to have; offer her the fanciest dessert and she would prefer, please, a plain red apple.

When the director of the Berkshire Museum proposed a cozy little gathering around a fireplace after the lecture in Pittsfield, a wealthy community full of potential backers of littérateurs, she replied, without apology or regrets, no. In answer to a question in the open forum there, instead of saying what her entire audience hoped to hear, she declared bluntly that she had failed to lay eye on any great American painting. In the Springfield Museum, which boasts of a few windowless galleries, she rubbed officials the wrong way by expressing a preference for windows, so that she could take a look outdoors between paintings. She was not currying favor with an audience of schoolteachers when she put or kept them in their place by stating that their business was to resist the changes in language which she was endeavoring to introduce. She even rejected an invitation from Hartford hopefuls, though they could remind her, and one did, that as sponsors of *Four Saints* they had pioneered in presenting her to the Connecticut valley.

No professional manager would have countenanced this highhanded treatment of audiences and sponsors, and few publicity-mad writers would have behaved as she did, either. It was not a smart thing for her to do. Many friends and admirers whom she might have won,

137

she simply didn't. She could have been obsequious, as her severest critics would have expected; she could have moved to a middle ground, quite safe and beyond reproach, accepting an invitation once in a while and sacrificing her plain red apple; instead, she was absolutely independent. She wasn't putting on an act, or being rude; she simply did not like parties, and she had her integrity to maintain. Few people have been so obsessed with a yearning for adulation, but in all my acquaintance with her, I never caught her conniving for it in a small or unworthy way; all her bids were big and splendid.

There were advantages in talking about *The Making of Americans* on the first night in Springfield, for an abridgment of the long novel had been translated into French by Bernard Faÿ. Formerly at Harvard and known in western Massachusetts, he was an academic link between the advanced writer and the lay public. That did not quite suffice to bring the two together. Miss Stein labored valiantly to explain that her story was essentially American, but sentences like the following were a little bewildering:

"This sense of a space of time and what is to be done within this space of time not in anyway excepting in the way that it is inevitable that there is this space of time and anybody who is an American feels what is inside this space of time."

A professor has recently contended that the lectures only too clearly betrayed that Miss Stein had nothing to say, yet the listeners at the fifteen which I attended thought she had something to say because, in the discussion periods, they remembered it, rephrased it, praised or challenged it. The most exciting feature of those evenings was the post-lecture arguments, which sometimes lasted an hour and were often as dramatic as the shipboard press conference. At such moments Miss Stein appeared at her best. Instead of remaining a lecturer, she became a superb conversationalist; instead of being an abstruse writer, she became a rich, living voice, a quick and entertaining wit, a warm personality. A touch of hostility in the questions served only to inspire her, and she was never stuck for an answer, even when, as at Mount Holyoke, it seemed as if part of the audience was ganging up on her.

At Johnson Chapel in Amherst, where President Stanley King and Mrs. King were her hosts, she talked on *Poetry and Grammar* and the verdict of the students, revealed by remarks as they filed out, was that "she knows what she's doing." No doubt her indifference to the rules of punctuation which might have bothered them made welcome sense.

She loved Deerfield, where I, as a former teacher in the academy, was able to serve as guide. She visited the John Williams house, was properly impressed by the door hacked by tomahawks, inspected a church with a beautiful old pulpit, and was regaled with unverifiable legends about a secret passageway and tunnel from the Colonial settlement to the river bank . . . "I always like to believe what I hear," she wrote in *Geographical History*. She would assure me later that Charlottesville "is a beautiful town but we like Deerfield better in spite of Mr. Jefferson, not that Mr. Jefferson did not do very well because he certainly did . . ." and she would recall how well the weather-worn buildings fitted the country-side and the elm-lined street: "They stand so well on the ground."

A Longmeadow friend hitched up a two-seater sleigh to drive Miss Stein and Miss Toklas through the winter woods. Bundled up in borrowed scarves, coats and caps, the women were as round as big and little barrels. The snow-laden branches, the smooth and silent ride and the crisp air delighted them; while warming up after-ward, Miss Stein was intrigued by the mysteries of her hostess' tack room.

An afternoon visit near Hartford was a pleasant experience, though Archibald MacLeish, who had been expected to be there, was absent. On the way back, with the snow getting deeper and the hour later until it was nip and tuck whether we'd reach Springfield early enough for a lecture that evening, the drifts finally piled so high that I jumped out and pushed. Luckily we arrived in the nick of time; Miss Stein, absorbed in the storm, the scenery and the driver's difficulties, seemed as indifferent to the prospect of being stalled as if she had no engagement before spring.

Another friend, who took Miss Stein and Miss Tok-las to Wesleyan, still recalls in detail a session in the public rooms of a fraternity house, where Miss Stein advised the boys gathered around her to enjoy books and pictures but not to feel they must analyze them, and where she silenced one questioner by declaring in effect: "I don't care to say whether I'm greater than Shakespeare, and he's dead and can't say whether he's greater than I am. Time will tell."

One evening at the Springfield *Union* Miss Stein and Miss Toklas watched a morning paper in process from reporters and deskmen to make-up, stereotyping and printing, and photographers took more pictures.

Miss Stein was fun to be with, and to observe being with other people. She liked plenty of time to herself, and perhaps required it, for though she had recovered from stage fright, the strain of being constantly under public scrutiny was still extreme. Being a celebrity, like being a genius, is a twenty-four-hour-a-day job. Wherever she appeared, she attracted attention, whether in railroad stations, bookstores, on the street or in a ladies' room—in a Providence hotel, this celebrity trained in continental frugality paid her own nickel and then offered to hold open the door to save the nickels of the others in her party.

When we entered public dining rooms, in Pittsfield, Northampton, Providence, some one would recognize her, introduce himself or send a note by a waiter asking for her autograph. She rarely refused such requests, for she loved to sign her name. If she didn't actually think in phrases tailored for guest-book and autograph purposes, she always had words ready as quickly as she could pick up a pen. I had seen her dash off something for the record in a museum in France with the speed with which she responded with her signature to pleas from clerks in a Springfield bookshop. Her numerous Chicago autographs were collected in a pamphlet; she

wrote in *Three Lives* for Mrs. Charles B. Goodspeed:
"To Bobsy Goodspeed three lives and as many lives always Gtde," and in *Four Saints* for Fanny Butcher:
"Dear Fanny you are the best of famous Fans and Famous, but the best the very best of Fannies, and always my affection Gtde."

Even taxi drivers knew her. One of them led me into a corner, asked if that was the famous Stein, said he missed *Four Saints* in Hartford and guessed he'd "wait till it gets in the movies, because the movies make them easier."

Miss Stein loved it all, it was "wonderful." She was the only person I ever knew who was deliriously happy for six successive months.

6

The first lunch at which we entertained Miss Stein and Miss Toklas was another one of those things like the near accident at the station. Our apartment looked out toward the Mount Holyoke range, friends said, or out over the railroad tracks, according to others. But since the tracks lay several blocks away, the choking smoke which filled the rooms when the guests arrived could not have blown in from passing trains.

Mrs. Kiddie was eager to have everything go smoothly; hosts to the most famous couple in the entire valley, she and I wanted to do it right. It was useful to learn that Miss Stein was fond of carrots, didn't eat citrus fruit or cheese, and always refused salt. But at my expense we also learned something about her manner of compounding literature.

One of our domestic problems was a gas oven which was as good a gas oven as the water heater at Bilignin was a good water heater. It went by fits and starts, and on this occasion some of our broiled chicken burned to a frazzle. What we wanted to do up brown we did up black. While Miss Stein and Miss Toklas walked hesitantly in the front door, sniffing, I sneaked the cinders out the back, crying over my shoulder that Mrs. Kiddie should "let this be a lesson to her."

It turned into a lesson for me, because the smoke required an apology and, since Miss Stein was involved, an explanation, and that included necessarily my scared exclamation, which Miss Stein committed to memory. She used it in *Everybody's Autobiography* and in conversation and letters, and when for a moment at the start of the war in 1939 there was a tentative plan for a second American tour, she hoped to taste once more "the cooking of Mildred, hope the stove has not been naughty again." That first meal was saved by the successful corn pudding, which started me to supplying the Bilignin gardener with seed.

It's a silly sort of story, and I naturally would rather not tell it. But when I asked Miss Toklas whether she objected to my writing this biography, she said, after of course not, that I must put in the let-this-be-a-lesson-to-you incident. Besides, it throws more light on Miss Stein. She thought our failure was fun. And my hasty remark was grist for her mill, and typifies an important ingredient in the making of her books.

The trip to Providence proved to be similarly instructive. Thanks to Mrs. Kiddie, who by this time had learned a lot about Miss Stein's likes, it developed into a lively party. It was a long, cold ride, and to while away the miles, Mrs. Kiddie started us to singing, first an old Welsh piece which she can't spell for me, then "Nous n'irons plus aux bois" and "My mother told me I never should play with Gypsies in the wood." My contributions were "La Madelon" and "Auprès de ma blonde." The most amazing success, however, was scored by radio commercials, principally "Yo ho yo ho yo ho yo ho, we are the makers of Wonder Bread," which Mrs. Kiddie remembered when we passed a billboard advertisement. Next to the "Lonesome Pine," that became Miss Stein's favorite.

Then there were the eggs. The New England sky reminded both visitors of the blue and white ceiling above Bilignin. The slippery roads and snowstorms which did not keep audiences at home did not keep Miss Stein and Miss Toklas at home, either. Driving one clear day out in the country, Miss Toklas spotted a lone patch of purple cloud, and pointed it out.

"Fresh eggs," replied Miss Stein.

"I said, look at that cloud," Miss Toklas insisted.

"Fresh eggs."

Miss Toklas asked: "Are you making symbolical language?"

"No," Miss Stein answered, "I'm reading the signs, I love to read the signs."

If the three phrases, "Let that be a lesson to you,"

"we are the makers of Wonder Bread" and "fresh eggs," represent part of Miss Stein's stock in trade, so does the mechanical listing of numbers particularly from one to ten. They all were built solidly into many of her portraits, poems, essays and stories.

"Numbers have such pretty names," she wrote in *Geographical History.* "It can bring tears of pleasure to ones eyes when you think of any number eight or five or one or twenty seven or sixty three or seventeen sixteen or eighteen or seventy three . . . in any language numbers have such pretty names." Paul Valéry's "M. Teste" felt poetry in numbers, too, though he preferred the large ones.

In book after book Miss Stein counts, adds, subtracts and multiplies. For example, under the title "An Instant Answer or A Hundred Prominent Men" [in *Useful Knowledge*], she enumerates them all, one, two, three, and so on, numbers but not names, and in one place she adds "one and one and one and one and one" and continues, fascinated, up to a hundred. Again we have *Four Saints in Three Acts;* besides "how many saints are there in it," the common how-many question which is encountered on numerous pages, the text includes passages of this sort:

> "Four saints are never three.
> Three saints are never four.
> Four saints are never left together.
> Three saints are never idle.
> Four saints are leave it to me.
> Three saints when this you see.

Begin three saints.
Begin four saints.
Two and two saints.
One and three saints."

In *Portraits and Prayers* we find:

"Forty make three run
Forty make four among
Thirty make twenty-two and bring
Twenty make five of twenty-one
And six make twenty-six and sung"

With equal frequency she used familar phrases culled from hide-and-seek, or riddles, or counting-off games; the ones which pleased her in her childhood, like "One little two little three little Indians, four little five little six little Indians," were copied carefully in a notebook. There were stereotypes such as "enough said" [in *Portraits and Prayers* and *Geographical History*], or roadside signs like "Come to Jesus" [in *Geographical History*], or adages such as "Least said soonest mended," "leave well enough alone" and "a little goes a long way" [all in *Geographical History*], or "in union there is strength" [*Portraits and Prayers*].

Cryptograms intrigued her, as if they imparted some additional magic to words. One in particular occurs again and again, either in the first person singular or the first person plural, and either written out, as "We understand you undertake to overthrow our undertaking," or presented in this form:

| stand | take | to | taking |
| we | you | throw | our |

It appears one or more times in *Portraits and Prayers*, *Everybody's Autobiography*, *The Mother of Us All*, where Thomson interprets it delightfully in music, and I don't know how many other books.

From hide-and-seek she borrows: "Red white and blue all out but you" [*Portraits and Prayers*], and from game songs: "Peas and beans and barley grow" [*Wars I Have Seen*], and "Ring around the Rosey" [*Four Saints* and *Geographical History*]. The old riddle, "black and white and read all over," is used in *Portraits and Prayers*. From Mother Goose comes "I am I because my little dog knows me" [*Geographical History*]. Children's contests suggested "One for the money two for the show three to make ready and four to go" [*Portraits and Prayers*]; "One two three all out but me" [*Four Saints*]; "One two all out but you three four shut the door" and "button button who has the button" [*Geographical History*].

She recalls "I see the moon and the moon sees me, God bless the moon and God bless me" [*Portraits and Prayers* and *Useful Knowledge*]; "one two three four five six seven, all good children go to heaven, some are good and some are bad, one two three four five six seven" [*Four Saints* and *Geographical History*]; "I do not know where I'm going but I'm on my way"; "left right left right left right, he had a good home when he left"; and an old phrase which she herself might have composed and which must have delighted her: "What you cannot eat you can" [all *Geographical History*].

In *Useful Knowledge* she repeats "star light star bright I wish I may I wish I might have the wish I wish

147

tonight" and "I wish I was a fish with a great big tail. A polly wolly doodle a lobster and a whale"—to which she immediately adds: "And I am certain no one is deceived." In "Capital Capitals," included in *Operas and Plays*, her characters play, or say they are playing, ring around a rosey, London bridge, High Spy.

One phrase amounted almost to an obsession with her. "When this you see remember me," the pretty thought which girls used to inscribe in autograph albums, is from one point of view just a sentimentality, written in a Spencerian hand, accompanied by sighs, blushes, averted eyes and intertwined fingers. Tracing it now through Miss Stein's pages, with Miss Stein dead for more than a year, it takes on a new, more poignant significance. To her, I think, it meant what it said; if it was nonsense, it was of a kind to hurt. It is a sad intimation of the mortality of which she was conscious, and when this I see I do remember her.

"It is a very fine sentence," she declared in *How to Write*, and she inserted it half a dozen times in *Portraits and Prayers* and one or more times in *Wars I Have Seen, Geographical History, Useful Knowledge, Four Saints, A Lyrical Opera Made by Two, Four in America*. Once in *Wars I Have Seen* it is dropped plumb in the middle of a sentence: "Today we were at Aix-les-Bains, end of July 1943 when this you see remember me, and in a kind of way it was different." In *A Lyrical Opera* we encounter it in this form:

> "When this
> You see
> Remember
> Me to she . . ."

Some of these rhymes, riddles, advertising slogans, plays on words, quips, jingles and the like, summoned from deep in her memories of the early years in San Francisco, occur in most of her works, and if not the whole, at least a part, as for instance "when this you see," half of the autograph-album sentence, is slipped in at unexpected places. It's like dumping into her published prose items copied from her scribbled shopping lists, such as "rosewater and glycerine," or notes from memo pads. She empties her mind's pockets into her pages, just as in fact she and Picasso once emptied their pockets into odd little piles on a table.

Mention of Picasso is not fortuitous. The artist used a similar device, as Thornton Wilder has remarked. Miss Stein's remembered phrases do for her prose what Métro tickets and newsprint did for the early cubist canvases on which they were pasted. They are not representation but the real thing; the rest of the prose and of the painting must bear the test of comparison with these stable and commensurable tabs.

7

"The train went along," Miss Stein the plane enthusiast commented critically after they returned to New York, "but that is about all that it did, but gradually it got here."

Springfield, she recalled, was good and peaceful, but in New York, "We don't seem to do anything but it goes on all day long . . . Yesterday afternoon I spent the whole day doing gramophone records and it was rather wonderful, it was out in the old Aeolian place and the new records are pretty wonderful, I did two sides of the Making, three portraits Matisse and Picasso and Sherwood Anderson and the first act of Madame Récamier . . ."

She consoled me for the rejection of a manuscript of mine by a publisher friend of hers: "Don't be dismayed books do and will come back but you just go on writing another one, the great thing is that writing should go on . . . And anyway go on starting another thing, when Alice fell off her horse the first time in California a total stranger said to her do you ever want to ride again Miss, and she said yes well he said then get right on him or you never will and it is just the same about mss. writing, so go to it, Kiddie, and if at first you don't succeed try try again, that is a sweeter spirit than let it be a lesson to you."

She reproached me for having chosen to praise in a new book a piece which I should have remembered reading in an earlier one: "You are nice kiddies but well you write me letters and mention the only thing in Useful Knowledge which was reprinted in Portraits and Prayers, and I say you are nice kiddies you are nice kiddies. There we are the makers of Wonder Bread and you are nice kiddies."

In New York for the last time, Miss Stein referred to a contract for the syndication of her articles:

"Oh and you will like hearing that although they did not sell my articles to many outside newspapers the Herald Tribune is very satisfied because the articles were enormously liked by the readers they care for most so

150

everybody is happy, we heard the records the gramophone records yesterday and that went off very well, so now we are shopping and next Saturday we are sailing on the Champlain, just the boat we came on, and so much has happened and it all has happened so naturally and it began with you . . . and so it is slowly unrolled and covering the continent in airplane is wonderful and we saw the ship leave for Honolulu and the mayor gave me a golden key of San Francisco, wood gold you know and here we are and most reluctant to say goodby to you and our native land."

From shipboard Miss Toklas assured us that "some day we'll come back and see the Kiddies and the Rock. Center and the Mississippi and Deerfield—but not California because G. hated it and even so Columbus Ohio is better than anything this side—the wrong side . . ." And then in conclusion, "The marvellous-marvellous-marvellous visit." And so it seemed to Miss Stein:

"Everything . . . was wonderful we were awfully moved, for it was wonderful and we knew it was wonderful every minute it was being wonderful and I did not really realize it was over until I suddenly said to Alice but now I have to be putting U.S.A. on the envelope and then I had a kind of shock of really knowing that it was really over."

There would have been a bit of the exile in Miss Stein even if she had never left America, for in her role as creative writer she stood off some distance from her subject matter, she practised aloofness, she required a perspective which Paris made available but which she would have discovered in Pittsburgh. By leaving her na-

151

tive land, she learned to embrace it the more closely. The idea of America as the "air-conditioned nightmare" which Henry Miller described so venomously; the expatriate's idea of gay Paree as a place for night life and unrestrained carousing; and the student's idea of Paris as historical and artistic monument . . . these ideas were completely alien to Miss Stein. She loved America the more dearly for seeing it from the rue de Fleurus, and her trip only confirmed her affection.

She told an Associated Press reporter in Paris: "Yes I am married; I mean I am married to America, it is so beautiful."

Still wearing the brown tweed and the braumeister's-deerstalker's cap, she continued:

"I am going back to America sometime, someday not too long. I am already homesick for America. I never knew it was so beautiful. It was like a bachelor who goes along fine for 25 years and then decides to get married. That is the way I feel, I mean about America."

$\mathcal{S}$ENTIMENTAL JOURNEY

1

AS SOON AS we were able to assure Miss Stein that we were going to France again in 1937, she rushed off a reply:

"Do you know what we are going to do we are going to drive ourselves to Avignon Arles St. Remy Les Baux and then sleep at Nimes and go to Uzes and St. Gilles and Aiguesmortes and Vienne and back to Bilignin and all the way Mrs. Kiddy will listen to the remembering of all of us and the very best time will be had by all, and Mrs. Kiddy instead of singing Wonder Bread will sing Nougat Nougat as we go in and out of Montelimar [which specializes in nougat], and as soon as you make up your mind let us know just when you are coming, won't it be wonderful to do all that together again and ci inclus [including] Mrs. Kiddy, I don't suppose you can find any Darling cigarettes but perhaps yes, who knows, and that will be nice. So that is settled . . . Lots of love lots of it and we will have a wonderful time."

Miss Toklas reminded her of a guide book: "Alice says bring the Guide Bleu of the region along, we only have a Michelin which only says hotels and nothing about beauty spots, we will have a wonderful time, we have all the maps so all we need is the songs, and the guide bleu, August is sacred to the kiddies happy kiddies and happy we . . ."

As soon as happy we reached Bilignin, we began to mull over plans for what Miss Stein described as our "sentimental journey." The trip of twenty years before was fresh in the memories of three of us, and the fourth was easily persuaded by our excited reminiscences and enthusiastic descriptions that we were going not to southern France but to Elysium. Like everyone else, we had grand fun looking forward to it right there without even rising from our chairs.

Miss Toklas' fun was diluted with work. She must have plans for the servants Madame Roux and Louise during our absence, must leave the house in order, must supervise the kitchen and keep us fed yet empty the larder so that there would be a minimum of waste. Moreover, she must assemble the special items of food, and sort out the clothes and toilet articles which she and Miss Stein would need to take with them. Days ahead of the departure she determined on an early start.

"Early," she emphasized in her crisp voice. We were sitting in the living room when she looked up from her knitting at Gertrude as if Gertrude were her enemy, and said:

"Early."

Everything was ready the night before. Miss Toklas and I had pored over maps, starred this town, X'ed that one, and compiled a list of distances in kilometres. The auto was polished, brushed out, greased, oiled and filled with gasoline; the suitcases were partly packed. By the latest and final arrangement we were to stay in Avignon for two nights rather than in Nîmes for one.

The problem was to prevent Miss Stein from scrapping the plan approved by us all, including herself, and on the spur of the moment doing something else. Four heads are not better than one if Miss Stein's is one. How could she decide today what she'd want to do tomorrow, or decide at home what she'd want to do on the road? She could not gainsay an itinerary which, after all, is only successive places in the course of a trip. But she opposed one drawn up in advance. She preferred to improvise, or to plan a minute ahead, the minute she arrived at a corner. Miss Toklas hoped to reach Châteauneuf-du-Rhône for lunch, and that meant covering a hundred miles in the morning. In order to do that we must start early, and we could not tinker with the prearranged itinerary.

Miss Stein would drive, I'd be at her side with maps, and Miss Toklas and Mrs. Kiddie were to sit in back. Sometimes Pépé was to ride with them, sometimes in front. Basket had already been entrusted to a veterinary in Aix-les-Bains.

Miss Toklas' insistence on an early start reminded us of the lapse of time between Miss Stein's waking and her appearance downstairs; her usual leisurely breakfast could delay lunch until dinnertime, and Miss Toklas, again eying Miss Stein, repeated:

"Early."

"But have I ever held you up?" Miss Stein asked, tapping the arm of her chair.

Miss Toklas said nothing.

"Have I ever held you up?"

Though the answer was yes, Miss Toklas, a subtle manager, would not commit herself. Miss Stein's mood of sweet reasonableness was not mistaken by Miss Toklas for a reasonable mood. Miss Stein constantly threatened to turn into rout the regular, smooth routine which her companion enjoyed. Blueprint a book and you spoiled it; blueprint a three-day trip and you spoiled it, too, Miss Stein believed. Miss Toklas knew better, and it was her task to keep the conflagration in the salon from consuming the kitchen, to trim the blaze yet not appear always to be fighting fire.

"I think we ought to start at nine," she suggested firmly.

"Nine is all right." Miss Stein sounded as if that hour above all others suited her best.

"Nine is a fine hour," Mrs. Kiddie and I agreed, timidly, equally eager to get going and to keep out of trouble.

"Start whenever you please," said Miss Stein, having heard enough of this early business. "Start at nine and I'll be ready. Nine is all right."

Her needles flashing and no doubt her eyes, too, though they were prudently lowered, Miss Toklas reiterated: "Early."

A national budget to balance or an army to run would be a fair test for the methodical Miss Toklas, but Miss Stein was no fair test for anyone. She burst through programs, shattered schedules, demolished plans. During our sentimental journey Miss Toklas would have to contend with the appeal of names of unknown, out-of-the-way towns glimpsed fleetingly on signposts, with the lure of a yellow melon, with the attraction of a distant hilltop which it would be senseless to visit and yet which would call irresistibly to Miss Stein's five or six, or seven or eight, senses, in short, with the unaccountable impulses which made Miss Stein a fascinating person up to the line where practical affairs intervened, and a problem beyond that. Where are the delights of a holiday without a creative mind, yet what becomes of holiday plans with one? Miss Stein must lunch on time, for instance, yet yield to her whims while she traveled. She expected to be able to do both; it was Miss Toklas' duty to reconcile her to the enjoyment of one of these alternatives. As Miss Stein wrote in *Portraits and Prayers,* "there is no greater pleasure than in having what is a great pleasure," and she couldn't very well know one until she saw one en route.

At the last obstinate "early," Miss Stein got up from her desk, passed the fireplace and reached the door between salon and garden. She filled the broad opening. Back to us and hands buried in the pockets of her skirt, she tipped her short-clipped gray head up toward the bright stars. She tramped back to the fireplace, hesitated and stopped. Balancing from one foot to the other—in a film new then an angry elephant tugging at its chains swayed from side to side just as she did—and with the fingers of one hand caressing the scalp over her broad temple, she announced positively, once and for all:

157

"Only of course I won't get up until eight. I wouldn't get up until eight no matter where I was going I wouldn't get up until eight."

Mrs. Kiddie and I stole glances at her and Miss Toklas, but said nothing. It wasn't a quarrel, it was just two ways of looking at a thing; they had inched up into these opposite positions and couldn't move any further. A dispute would have been embarrassing; this was exciting.

Miss Toklas had the last word:

"We must start as early as we can."

On that, we went to bed.

In the morning we were ready to leave at half-past ten. The luggage was packed in the carrier. Miss Toklas delivered final instructions to Louise while Mrs. Kiddie and I waited for her. Miss Stein shoved hastily behind the wheel, settled herself and declared:

"Here I am, and where is everyone else?"

It was the sort of victory at which a five-year-old exults, and Miss Toklas, recognizing it at its worth, busy since five-thirty and as tired of trying to move a mountain as anyone else would have been, took an entire minute to open her door, plant one foot and then the other on the running board, pull herself up to the floor of the car, step inside, turn, begin to sit, sit, reach for the door, grasp the handle, pull it, and then lean back. Mrs. Kiddie and I hopped in as fast and as mum as we could, I with a handful of maps. Pépé nestled beside Miss Stein; since he was the only one of us who had not bothered her about an early start, she stroked his ears and back tenderly.

The auto stood in the courtyard between the village

road and the house. Louise had already swung the great iron gate wide open and cautiously flattened herself against the stone wall. Madame Roux had left her washing and, hands wrapped in her apron, smiled us a bon voyage.

Now Miss Stein was galvanized into action. Just as, instead of merely mouthing her arguments, she was accustomed to shake her head dramatically, wave the words out with her arms and march back and forth to press home her points, so starting the car was not merely a calm, mechanical reaching of a foot for a button. She shifted briskly in her seat. Both hands clamped down hard on the wheel, her whole magnificent torso stiffened, she leaned forward excitedly and her head dropped farther between her shoulders as a wrestler's might to guard against a stranglehold.

That electric spirit charged all the rest of us, with the possible exception of Miss Toklas. Mrs. Kiddie laughed loudly. Pépé sprang to his feet and his ears perked up. I held onto the maps for dear life. Madame Roux wagged her apron, Louise called and waved and jumped up and down, and we shot out through the gate. It was as thrilling as the first airplane flight.

The sun was high but not hot. The traffic was not heavy. Setting out in the valley of the upper Rhône, we arrived at the river itself, Miss Stein's favorite river, within a few kilometres. Between the lines of rounded willows and pointed poplars, we caught rushing glimpses of tall white cliffs rising from the further bank. A detachment of Algerians from a near-by barracks crowded closer together. A team of swaying oxen was poked and hirrupped off into the ditch out of our car's way.

Though we could not loiter, there were pleasant breaks. In St.-Marcellin we stopped for patisserie, tiny crisp dough boats packed with paste having a lemon tang; paper-thin, chocolate-covered cookies; fluffy and flaky tidbits with vanilla flavoring; and some plainer fare, all of which we ate without slackening our speed. If it was to be itinerary versus pastry, I gladly would have torn up the one and gobbled up the other.

Market day delayed us at Romans. The main street was closed to autos. Ripe fat blue figs, yellow and red plums, large yellow melons running with juice, pears both pink and yellow, blue, purple and pearl-colored grapes in sculptured clusters, and cloth, pottery, tin-ware, kitchen utensils, brushes, brooms and innumerable other articles on stands or on the ground were spread all over the square, the walks and the pavement, and overflowed around the side and across the front of the church.

Its fine, bare façade dated from the twelfth century, and some beautiful unornamented pillars in the interior from the thirteenth. We parked close to the thick old walls and wandered inside. Miss Stein, wishing she had a flashlight with which to probe some of the dark corners above us, remembered an architectural student who had difficulty persuading the French that the beam of his pocket light was not harming the building or violating the law. Yet hard as it was to see, she located the box for Saint Anthony and dropped in a coin, as she always did, for this patron saint of those who, like Miss Toklas, lose things or mislay them.

She bought no melons, though the sight of them put an idea in her head. Even Miss Toklas, more mindful than the rest of us of the mileage still to go before lunch, was beguiled by the colorful displays. We stared wide-eyed at the townspeople, in corduroys, aprons, kerchiefs, wooden shoes, and they stared wide-eyed at us, and, and it was time, Pépé had his first walk, or doodle as it was called.

We drove down the long white main street of Montélimar, singing as per schedule, and stopped for nougat. Mrs. Kiddie brought a couple of small packages back to the car, and Miss Stein, who believed in armfuls rather than handfuls, fished in her pocket and urged:

"Here, Mildred, take more money and buy more nougat."

At two o'clock, well behind time, we reached Châteauneuf-du-Rhône. There Miss Toklas had expected to find a good restaurant but she had forgotten the name of it. I must not ask for the best restaurant, Miss Stein insisted, but use the formula: "Where can we eat well in this town?" When I tried this phrase on a gentle, oldish man watching a young boy repair a bicycle in the shady edge of an orchard, he ambled over to the car, rested one foot on the running board and one hand on the window ledge, and assured us confidentially that we couldn't.

By the looks of things he was right, and Miss Toklas made the damaging admission that she might have confused this Châteauneuf with several others.

We started on, and missed a corner, inevitably. Miss Stein would drive right past all the signs where they might be read to the center of an intersection where

they no longer could be, and then demand breathlessly:
"Where do I go now? Tell me quickly! Kiddie!"

Now she kept turning the auto in the most tempting directions, hoping to catch a wrong road before the right one could be identified. Never prepared for her question, which usually jumbled my wits, I made a blind guess, and in two minutes we entered a narrow suspension bridge across the Rhône. Every place on the day's original itinerary lay on the east side, where we were, but the causeway was not wide enough for Miss Stein to back around. Anyway, even Miss Toklas weakened before the splendid view. The river's broad flow was split by a dazzling white sandbar, with a swift current near us and a slower one beyond. Downstream on the left, high, rusty cliffs, scored in beautiful abstract patterns, sprang straight out of the water.

Viviers rose directly before us. On the right, a lofty rampart, wall and a cathedral with a Romanesque tower and nave crowned another soaring cliff. Ahead of us there was an episcopal palace dating from the seventeenth century and beside it a hotel built under Louis XV. Behind these eminences lay the red-tiled roofs of the town, swept the year round by the mistral, the sort of wind which kept Miss Toklas tight in the car with the windows shut while the rest of us ran off sightseeing. She said she loved a view but liked to sit with her back to it.

Miss Toklas may have preferred not to stop, but not so Miss Stein and not so the Kiddies. It was a lucky mistake. Viviers, new to us all, proved to be the most interesting place added to the violated itinerary.

162

"Where do we eat well?" brought the reply: a little restaurant near the town's further limit. A woman knitting occupied a bench in the shade of a tree, the breeze rumpling her gray hair. Some girls ooo-la-la'ed about our miniature dog. We climbed three steps to. a small porch where a bicyclist with clips around the cuffs of his pants was cleaning his teeth with a pointed pick. He studied us intently one after the other as if he were the visitor and we were the zoo. Ducking our heads, we entered by parting the slender chains which, hanging close together from the top of the doorway, kept out flies without swinging too violently in the wind.

There were front and back rooms, the first café and the second restaurant. A young waitress approached, withdrew, returned with another and the proprietress herself. Talking ceased behind them, burst forth loudly among us. The proprietress determined to seat us in the back room and pointed the way. Miss Toklas, after carefully inspecting light, air, view and general comfort, preferred the place where we were. The proprietress insisted that other people ate in the restaurant and so could we. Miss Toklas declared emphatically for the café. Miss Stein thought it didn't matter. Of course it did, Miss Toklas maintained. We stayed where we were.

There was no merlan, or white bait, for which Miss Stein had been working up an appetite ever since morning, but to make up for it we were served rich coarse bread baked in the village, shells of fresh sweet butter, a country wine, chicken and freshwater crabs with a delectable sauce which aroused Miss Toklas' enthusiasm. It aroused her ire, too, for it occasioned another set-to with Miss Stein. The composure with which Miss Stein moved through this world and this life was disturbed most often by events relating to the dogs. For their sake she could forget her scruples; she would not cheat or fib for literature, love or money, but she would for Pépé and Basket. Pleasures denied to her she enjoyed vicariously through them, and she could submit to some social disciplines all the more resignedly as she allowed the dogs to disregard them. Careful as could be about her own diet, she fed them everything they liked; no doubt she was better able than the rest of us, with our unresponsive palates, to understand how much fun it was to eat unwisely. If Pépé or Basket was too greedy, Miss Toklas could guess why.

Pépé, in Miss Stein's lap, was snapping at every piece of bread offered him, and it looked suspicious since a quantity of dry bread was not likely to appeal to him. Miss Toklas suggested innocently:

"Don't you want me to take Pépé?"

"No. Why should I want you to take Pépé?"

"Isn't he eating a lot of bread?"

"He's eating a lot of bread because he's hungry," Miss Stein declared without however daring to meet her companion's glance. Then out popped the secret:

"I put just a little sauce on it."

She spoke nonchalantly, what was a speck of sauce, a dab like that, holding up her little finger, not enough to see. But there was a sheepish look on her face.

Miss Toklas laid down the law: "He must eat his bread without sauce."

"He won't eat it without sauce! If he won't eat it

without sauce, he'll starve. It's not so bad to sicken as to starve!"

With her head thrown back, Miss Stein burst into a huge laugh intended to settle all objections and to mask her own discomfiture as well. Above the red and white oilcloth table cover, boldly where all of us could see, she offered Pépé a last bite.

"Well all right take him," she surrendered finally, and stopped looking like a boy caught stealing jam. Miss Toklas did not acknowledge her triumph by even a flick of an eye; perhaps self-control had become a habit.

After lunch we walked along alleys, selected picture postcards, and climbed up to the churchyard where stubby, froglike ancient cannon squatted in a row, their mouths agape.

At Orange, next stop back on our own side of the Rhône, while Miss Toklas napped in the car and Mrs. Kiddie and I clambered over the magnificent Roman theatre, Miss Stein went walking and returned with a melon, a yellow one weighing about four pounds. Hugging it under her arm as she crossed the vast, dust-blown square, she passed it to us to pinch the ends and judge whether it was ripe.

"I think it's a good one," she announced.

If she bought a melon, it could be expected to be more flavorsome than anyone else would buy, just as, if she wrote a book, it would be better than anyone else's. Since the purchase intruded on Miss Toklas' domain, however, I suspect she did not approve, and I do not remember her agreeing that it was ripe. Anyway, as she scorned sheep not raised on salt meadows, so she scorned melons not grown in Spain.

At a near-by shop I got a crude jackknife. Several kilometres out of the city, Miss Stein swung off the route nationale in search of a secluded spot. It always seemed curious to me that for a picnic she parked a mile off the road, but that the edge of a main highway sufficed as a substitute for the ubiquitous American comfort station. When I commented to Miss Toklas that this proved how French they had become, she adroitly gave me half an answer: not at all, she explained, back in California in her youth they always picnicked way out of sight of the road.

No sooner had Miss Stein decided, "There, that's the place we're hunting for," and turned into it across flat stubble, than Miss Toklas observed dryly:

"This looks to me like a dump."

"It will end soon," she was assured.

It ended after five minutes of bumping along a pair of wheel tracks; even then, the memory of the smell remained, and there were rusty tin cans which were hard to dodge when we backed out.

"What's the matter with this?" the driver asked in a tone which warned us that the only acceptable answer was nothing.

And nothing really was. The highway was too far away for the noise of traffic to carry or passersby to see us. In the distance, gentle Mont Ventoux rose protectingly behind Avignon. Low bushes helped to screen us, and sprigs of wild lavender waved prettily above the stunted, yellow grass.

166

Like a center over a football, I crouched on the ground with the melon and my team went into a huddle around me. Juice followed the knife in a steady stream for eighteen inches from end to end, and in lifting out the first delicious slice, I uncovered a matted nest of gold seeds. We ate it dripping off our chins, and praised it to the skies, not because we wanted to please Miss Stein but because it was superlatively fine. Our enthusiasm, I suspect, started her to buying more.

Maybe that first one was so good because she worked on it. If a godmother could turn a coach into a pumpkin, Miss Stein's incantations, more exotic than those in fairy stories, could produce a perfect texture and an incomparable flavor; certainly it did the melon no harm to be carted across the warm square at Orange in her arm, patted with her thick sun-browned fingers and rubbed with the palm of her hand.

At Avignon we settled comfortably in the Hôtel d'Europe, and went out to eat in a restaurant. Miss Toklas, who was tired, took Pépé back to their room. Miss Stein, Mrs. Kiddie and I walked out by the light of a moon a hair's thickness from full. The Palace of the Popes was both milk white and deep black, and from its high gardens the Rhône was a shiny silver. Frenchmen on the benches by the winding walks argued about the gold supply, or made love, or sat in lonely, contented silence smoking a pipe or burning a cigarette down to the last eighth of an inch. The air was cool and quiet. Except for a hurrying soldier, a man on a bicycle, and a fellow limping along with a cane, there was little activity in the streets, which were dark beyond the circle of feeble light at the corners and the rays which spread out from one or two cafés. A few girls and women in kimonos or less, one of them bargaining with a customer, waited in the doorways of the district through which we passed on our way back.

We talked about the papal residence, the placid Rhône, the sights we'd seen that day and the ones we planned to see the next. Though Miss Stein was sixty-three that summer, she walked with the unflagging vigor of a person many years younger, and she was full of ideas for new books, one of which she described:

"I want to write a novel about publicity, a novel where a person is so publicized that there isn't any personality left. I want to write about the effect on people of the Hollywood cinema kind of publicity that takes away all identity. It's very curious, you know, very curious the way it does do just that." . . . The novel was *Ida.*

The hotel lights were frugally lowered when we entered the lobby again. Miss Stein carried a small bottle of Vichy water up to her room, and we were sure she wouldn't be awake before eight.

Nevertheless we started an hour earlier the next morning, perhaps because a little donkey with a huge bray trotted under her window as well as ours shortly after dawn. Les Baux, the hilltop town converted into a museum, was our first stop. With Miss Toklas again hiding safely away from the mistral inside the closed auto, three of us wandered off in all directions. The only residents were a handful of guides and their families. We admired the painted ceiling of an old refectory, poked through ruined palace and church, and enjoyed the superb views, but stayed prudently off the topmost stairs, as steep as ladders and guarded only by rickety railings, which led up to the dizzy heights where the blasts of wind seemed strong enough to knock a man off his feet.

Miss Stein, remembering, I don't know how, that three years before when she visited us we had left up our Christmas tree for her, bought a tiny ox and sheep with which to decorate our next one—now a tree would hardly be our tree without those pale clay miniatures snuggled at the foot of it.

Picture-taking, which Miss Stein loved, began in earnest at the base of the old Roman arch at St.-Rémy. After crossing the Rhône again, not by mistake but to look back at the riverfront from the Tarascon of Daudet's *Tartarin*, we headed for Arles and lunch. The place where we ate well here, it turned out, was a restaurant in a shady thoroughfare lined with plane trees. A boy in short short pants who offered to take our order was either frightened by our insistence on details or stumped by our French.

"There's a soup and a meat and two vegetables," he began.

"What soup?" asked Miss Toklas.

"A soup and a meat," his shrill voice repeated a little less confidently.

Miss Toklas interrupted severely: "I understand. We may have a soup. Bon! Now I ask you, what soup?"

The youngster, who wasn't as big as Miss Toklas, gave up and ran off. At once a man appeared, with long involuted mustaches, heavy broad shoulders and tattooed arms more like a stevedore's than a cook's, so fierce-looking that I couldn't decide whether he intended to avenge his son or merely take our order.

Miss Stein then called for a wider chair, and that obliged us all to shift almost as if for a fifth person. On the approach of a dog bigger than Pépé, as all dogs are, Pépé had to be grabbed up out of danger. Next I returned to the car for hard crackers for Miss Stein and and black bread for Miss Toklas and me. The last thing was to turn Pépé over to Miss Toklas who, then settled and not so cross as she had been, was free to tell the proprietor, also much more amiable than he had seemed, the particulars of our appetites.

The menu, written in the usual purplish ink and the familiar ornate script, included the long awaited merlan.

"I'll have merlan," Miss Stein exclaimed quickly before anyone could oppose her. "Who else wants merlan?"

Mrs. Kiddie did.

"Horrible fish," Miss Toklas remarked.

If Mrs. Kiddie wanted to placate Miss Stein, I'd placate Miss Toklas; but if it was as good as the other dishes, and it looked it served with tail tucked in mouth, I regret my choice.

Discovering more melons after lunch, Miss Stein bought two herself and inveigled me into buying another. When I returned from the arena and theatre, I was told it was in a store a step down the street, where I must come and inspect it. Though it was the biggest we had seen, she confided out of Miss Toklas' hearing that it ought not to cost more than six francs. It proved to be a giant, the size of a watermelon, weighing over seven pounds, with patches of a dull grass-green over which had burst sun-yellow streamers, like a field of grain, brilliant colors which would have delighted Van Gogh, who had indeed feasted his eyes on them in the same city. I paid seven and a half francs.

I was drawn into this business, I figured, because Miss Stein didn't care to accept the responsibility for filling the back of the car with more melons than we could eat in a week. As a matter of fact, Miss Toklas never complained about them. One explanation is that she was charitable; another, that she knew it wouldn't do any good. However, it is to be noted that in an antique shop in the same street she ran across some fine old glass, called me in to gloat over it with her, and bought a piece. If that wasn't a rebuke to Miss Stein, it was sufficient consolation to Miss Toklas.

We took more pictures in front of Saint Gilles' beautiful Romanesque church. After rolling across the flat, warm Camargue along roads with a double screen of high hedges which made blind corners out of the right-angle turns, we reached walled Aiguesmortes, its stifling, breathless square adorned with a statue of St.-Louis, who used the town as a base for a crusade. There, while I drank beer and mopped my brow, my three companions tried pomegranate juice and pretended to like it.

We arrived in Nîmes in time to explore the Roman gardens, peer down into the ancient baths and hurry up the steep paths to the Tour Magne, but too late in the afternoon for an appropriate celebration. The next day on a last brief visit we saw the great arena and the Maison Carrée, and paused for a few minutes in front of the Hôtel du Luxembourg where three of us had stayed twenty years before. We took photographs on the broad sidewalks, and I went in for one glance around the lobby, which did not look familiar. Miss Stein and Miss Toklas stayed outside.

After making only one addition to our private melon collection, we sped off to Remoulins and the Pont-du-Gard. The restaurant was about a hundred and fifty feet downstream from the greatest of Roman monuments. The narrow, rocky Gard bends sharply at the aqueduct between two shoulders of hills; the shadows deepen early in the evening, and the air turns cool. Miss Stein had promised us a full moon at this very spot, and she produced one . . . melon-shaped.

Soon after we had begun dinner, it rose through the treetops across the river, lifted higher and finally shone on the entire face of the handiwork of Romans almost two thousand years old. The pearly light and the black shadows magnified the enormous arches of the two lower tiers and outlined the smaller, delicate ones which carry the channel for water.

Horace, Virgil and Catullus entered the conversation. What had they done, it was argued, comparable to the Pont-du-Gard, this eloquent testimony to the genius of Rome. Only one writer, Julius Caesar, had come near matching the grandeur of the engineer. The vigor of the republic and the early empire, which had spread the Tiber city's fame throughout the Mediterranean world and north through three-part Gaul, was symbolized perfectly in this soaring structure, so solid that the French building a modern road across the valley backed it up against Rome's enduring arches. Miss Stein wished Thornton Wilder were there to hear, for he had been defending the Latin poets, she said. A lover of poetry, he would also have been a reliable judge of bridges.

After dinner we started for Avignon. A dance in a village square delayed us. Torch lights were set in the gutters, violins scraped and accordions bleated louder than the sound of our motor, and young couples wound gaily around us and back and forth in front of us and slowed the car nearly to a stop.

On the last day of the journey the Stein-Toklas conflict was intensified to its most dramatic pitch. While few people question Miss Stein's genius, not so much has been heard about Miss Toklas'. If the one is the creative spirit, the other is the immensely practical spirit.

"We live simply and we eat well," Miss Stein wrote in the Toklas *Autobiography*. To succeed in this, they had put up an unremitting struggle; to a lax world they presented an impregnable front which was contrived largely by Miss Toklas. She was manager and captain of the team, called the plays, ran interference, decided when the grounds were too wet for a game, even acted as cheer leader. It was she who told me, when the time came, that I should say Alice, not Miss Toklas, and Gertrude, too.

If the partnership was unconquerable when it faced

outsiders, each woman was unconquerable when confronting the other. To find out what happens when an irresistible force meets an immovable object, it was necessary merely to watch these two. Sometimes one gave way, sometimes the other, but sparks flew always. It was a perverse attraction. The give and take, not so much of spoken words as of concealed surges of will, of stubborn forces beneath the placid surface of one almost inscrutable countenance and the other, was like a battle of natural elements. Unless you wanted to get hurt, you ducked.

The trip home, then, was again through Nîmes and on to Uzès. Its centers of interest included an admirable Hôtel du Baron de Castille, a crypt where harried Christians once hid, the château and a curious little square with arcades supported by enormous pillars— our car bounced along behind the pillars though I am sure that was sidewalk instead of highway. The cathedral, beyond which stands a vine-covered pavilion where Racine supposedly did some writing, is surrounded on three sides by alleys of wide, thick chestnut trees shading a promenade which overlooks the beautiful valley of the Alzon river. A défense de circuler sign nailed to a post warned plainly:

"Vehicles not allowed beyond this point."

Sign or no sign, Miss Stein intended to drive around there for the sake of both pavilion and view. Miss Toklas opposed this violation of the regulation.

"I don't want you to do it," she declared, invoking law and order against the natural-born lawbreaker.

Miss Stein insisted.

"Then I'll walk!" Miss Toklas rolled a couple of melons out of the way and leaned suddenly toward the door.

"No, no, no, no, don't be silly. We're in the car, it's smooth, it's level, it's like a road, it might as well be a road, it is a road!"

She hunched forward in her seat, gripped the wheel, shifted gears and we leaped ahead. If she could do as she pleased with pen and paper, why not with a five-passenger sedan? Defiance was a habit, and the rebel in the study was the rebel on the road. The lovely vista and the ancient door of the low, square pavilion were worth the risk, or would have been if we couldn't have seen them any other way, and Miss Stein discussed them volubly. That gave Miss Toklas no chance for a fresh outburst, but she had finished with her objections, anyway; she never nagged.

Now it was time to hunt for a real picnic spot. We were supplied with a roast chicken, ripe figs, oranges, bread and pastry, and melons enough for a regiment. We needed wine, said Miss Toklas. But we were traveling well away from the towns as we cut back toward the broad valley of the Rhône. After some miles, Miss Stein sighted a weather-worn, gray village with an encircling wall, and we, or she, decided in a jiffy that we could buy wine there. Miss Toklas preferred the main road; we might hit bad bumps, she warned, or a steep, narrow and extremely hazardous road.

That was exactly what we struck: a steep, narrow and extremely hazardous road, with bad bumps. Miss Stein herself had had enough by the time we reached the

175

edge of the village, half a mile from the highway. On foot I climbed up to the deserted, silent square, where I bought some very ordinary vin ordinaire in a café in which I was the only customer. Meanwhile, a peasant and two old women had appeared from a house near where the others were waiting, complained about the need for rain, presented a bottle of wine, and sold Miss Stein four more melons.

Miss Toklas didn't know what we'd do with them all in Bilignin; without a truck I didn't know how we'd even get them there. Some wrapped in newspaper and some not, they jammed the luggage carrier and rolled on the floor of the car under our feet. I have no idea what became of all of them. We gave one to Madame Pierlot, we ate them at Bilignin for meal after meal, and when Mrs. Kiddie and I returned to Paris we could spare a big one for the proprietress of our hotel. None was wasted. I am sure.

While Miss Toklas' disapproval of the change from sentimental journey to foraging party was perfectly understandable, so too, if you were familiar with Miss Stein, was her openhanded purchasing. With melons as with everything else, there couldn't be too much of a good thing; if one was good, all the melons in the Midi were better. She enjoyed every bite, hers but even more ours. This time she had the last word, and Miss Toklas must have been glad, for it was loving and generous. In *Portraits and Prayers* she wrote:

"To introduce a melon, two melons, to introduce two melons, sugared melons candied melons to them, to introduce them to produce for them to send to them a

176

melon to send them to send melons two melons to them, this makes them give you their blessing."

That adds up to only a dozen or so melons, and we had many more than that. But it does make us give to her our blessing. We admire people for noble character or great wisdom, but we're apt to grow fond of them just because of different traits, because of the foolish little things they do. Creative ability in the raw, impersonal, hard and forceful, is nothing to inspire affection, and it is impossible to caress; that's for Miss Stein's public to respect. Miss Stein's friends loved her because among other peccadilloes she bought enough melons for a fruit store, because she spoiled Basket and Pépé, because she was so vain about being photographed, because she must have merlan, because she was such a trial to Miss Toklas—and Miss Toklas' troubles were still to be stretched over several hundred kilometres this last day of the trip.

After lunch in a field by a stone wall and hedge we drove to the Rhône and turned up the west bank. Sunday afternoon and balmy weather brought out endless lines of bicyclists. In one town a flag-draped stand, sideshow, bands, speeches, crowded streets and innumerable gendarmes marked a celebration by war veterans. Château after château, some of them colorless skeletons silhouetted against the blue sky and some tumbled in almost complete but genteel ruin with a genuine Middle-Aged respectability, crowned successive hilltops and made the Rhône valley the rival of the picturesque and romantic Rhine.

Still seventy-five kilometres from home when night

177

fell, we stopped at the café des Pyramides in Vienne for a memorable dinner of pâté, écrevisses, chicken with truffles, salad, a "bombe" of ice cream, petits fours, fruits, almonds in their green hulls, and coffee. Pépé was held in one lap after another while several shaggy Pyrenees dogs, the size of Newfoundlands, padded softly around on the painted soil of the open-air restaurant.

The rest of the ride developed the last phase of the battle royal. As if she foresaw the issue over which the fight would be waged, like a smart general outguessing his foe, Miss Toklas remarked suddenly that it was always necessary to be supplied with maps, they were absolutely indispensable. Yet what, she continued, was the use of having them if a person didn't follow them?

Miss Stein felt no assurance at all that the cartographer can transfer to a square, flat paper even an approximation of the relative positions of towns, some on a hill and some in a valley, and change a poplar-shaded, winding road under a full moon into a red-pencil line. Even if a cartographer could, perhaps he wouldn't wish to; an expressionist or cubist mapmaker, as Miss Stein would appreciate, could raise hob with the apparent realities registered by the unsophisticated eye.

Whatever the reason, she liked her own brand of geography. We were on the right road to Belley and Bilignin, at least according to Michelin, when out of the dark at a crossing loomed a signpost pointing to Crémieux.

"There," Miss Stein exclaimed, slowing down, "Crémieux, that's the place!"

Miss Toklas was not caught napping: "What place, if you please?" she demanded in a flash.

"Where we want to go."

"We do not want to go to Crémieux! Kiddie!"—in an urgent appeal—"Isn't Crémieux off our road?"

I acknowledged that it was.

"Hmmm?" Miss Stein commented grudgingly.

"You see!" Miss Toklas cried to us triumphantly. "Gertrude wants to go to Crémieux when it's way off our road!"

Miss Stein laughed. "Well, I'd like to go to Crémieux, yes."

She hated to give in. Behind the wheel for hours on end, the tireless woman should have been content at midnight to go straight home, get the trip over with and tumble into bed. I could catch a glimpse of her occasionally as we passed under a street lamp or as the road turned and the moon shone into her side of the auto. She sat low in the seat, right hand on the wheel, right foot on the accelerator and the other flat on the floor, hitting a speed of thirty-five to forty miles an hour. She had the profile of one of the Romans who had built Nîmes, Orange and Arles, yet in her eyes was an un-Roman yearning for Crémieux.

This name which she had probably never heard before exercised some inexplicable fascination, unless it was just an excuse for staying out late. Without maps, sailing along in the night through rare wisps of mist, who could be positive that Crémieux was not on our way?

It was as if Miss Stein's practical sense had been

179

removed from her person and deposited in the person of Miss Toklas. The ego was in the front seat, and the alter ego in the back. The battle which most geniuses fight within themselves was exteriorized and fought openly between her and her friend. They were dear enemies; they had to have each other, but the compulsion in it sometimes fretted them. In a way, they had been enemies not merely for the thirty years they had lived together, but always.

It was half-past midnight, and we were determined to go to Bilignin, not Crémieux. Given one more sign, we might have failed, but Miss Stein was spared that temptation and we were spared the ultimate struggle. I was glad Miss Toklas won. But I hoped in another year we could set out on a pilgrimage to Crémieux. It is sad to watch one friend score a victory which another friend loses.

So WE DO NOT KNOW QUITE WHAT WE ARE DOING

1

"WELL HERE is peace, at least for twenty years," a French soldier reassured Miss Stein soon after the first World War, and she would have believed him if he had said it twenty years later, on the eve of Hitler's invasion of Poland. No war cloud was so black but that she could find a silver lining. Her conviction that peace would endure persisted right up to the minute when it was broken.

Times were uncertain. There was a depression; Spaniards flew at the throats of one another and of German and Italian invaders; il Duce blustered into Albania, needled the French in Africa and Corsica; der Führer made ugly noises; battle raged in the Far East. These were troubles, but were they portents? Miss Stein and Miss Toklas had had their war, and it was a cataclysm of the first magnitude; they were willing to believe that lightning wouldn't strike twice in the same generation.

Hitler's loud mouth did not sound to them as menacing as the rattle of the Kaiser's sword.

In the winter of 1934–35, Miss Toklas wrote that Paris would be spared disturbances "if our friends are to be trusted. We are not going to have a king, nor communism, nothing but a little more taxes."

Nevertheless, she added: "I've been sending all Gertrude's unpublished work to Carl Van Vechten in N.Y. fearing that some day we might have to leave '27' [rue de Fleurus] and them and that was an unbearable thought. He wrote and said he would take care of them, but wouldn't it [the new war or revolution] perhaps get there before it came here."

In reply to a remark of mine that a mechanical strike on my paper was over, Miss Stein "was glad . . . that you are once more at peace everybody tries to be at war but they really do not'pull it off very well, they do continue to be more or less at peace, after all after everybody has done a really big war it is not so easy to do it again, and so after all they are at peace."

War, she seemed to imply, was a major achievement, and though the super-race of her time, the giants of the early years of the century, had possessed the fortitude to start one and carry it through, she doubted whether the new generation could manage it. So then she reverted to tamer topics:

Hazel nutting was "lots of fun and diverts ones mind gently and firmly from Spain and principally France . . . Picasso is in Majorca and worries about Spain, [artist William] Cook was evacuated from Palma and wrote rather wonderfully about it, Blum is scared and nobody except the royalists seem to know what they want and they probably won't get what they want so there it is."

The fact that within one letter she felt obliged to move from nutting to Blum and France's severe internal strain indicated how insistent political and economic events were becoming. Yet in reporting on a secret rally of the reactionary Croix de Feu, she ignored the ill omen and noted only the drama:

"My but everything is xciting, here in Belley imagine it they had a meeting of 10000 croix de feu and it was organized just mysteriously like the Middle ages a little boy came around with a litttle piece of paper and on it it said meet at such a place, and there a man with a handkerchief waved them somewhere, and they came and they had loud speakers to direct them and they had wagons of essence [gasoline] to revital them [for supplies] and my gracious we knew nothing about [it] until two days after, we were mushrooming [gathering mushrooms] in another direction. That is the way revolutions are."

That is also the way revolutions are brought about. But many people besides Miss Stein were caught mushrooming in 1939, 1940 and 1941. It was more agreeable than war, or thoughts of war, especially to tired and vulnerable Europeans. They dreaded the horrors of war, they yearned for the satisfactions of peace. One well-known artist, whose name Miss Stein asked me not to reveal, communicated with her about the bloody civil war which was rending his native land, and his letter said:

183

"All I want is to live in the country with my wife and children."

She herself confessed: "I guess I have lost interest in world politics in newspapers and in sides, if they would only leave us alone in our little lost places, it will have to come to that again."

The repeated return of Madame Pierlot's son Robert to the Maginot Line as the Führer threw hapless France into one fright after another shocked Miss Stein deeply, and she was no less disturbed when village boys and farmers' sons, her friends and neighbors, followed him off to service. But the unease and menace still had their picturesque aspects, or perhaps she supposed merely that they interested me:

The Chasseurs Alpins in new clothes were quartered in Belley and "Gamelin came and reviewed them, they had a micro arranged to catch the words that fell from him and none fell."

Or again: "We are in full panoply of war [1936] so we do not know quite what we are doing, 2500 reservists are doing their 28 days in Belley and we have 28 in the barn and in the usual way of the army they spend the day taking out the things they have brought in and bringing in the things they have taken out, but you know all about that. I said to the colonel but why do they not tent in the fields and he said solemnly a french soldier should always sleep with a roof over him and I said why and he said because otherwise they might get rheumatism and what then would their relatives say about that."

By the end of the month the detachment had packed

up and left, and Belley was again "a deserted country town." It was the picture that fascinated her, and not the significance. A novelist instead of a politician, she studied the human aspects of the uncertain times, the color of troop movements, the reaction of native Bilignites to the constant alarms. Headlines had ceased to bother her, but she never failed to ask how they affected her neighbors. In her eyes the function of a colonel began and ended when he had explained to her how and why a soldier avoided rheumatism.

Stubbornly and perhaps ungenerously, I demanded more of her. Another correspondent would have been content with her delightful anecdotes; for the moment I was less absorbed in long-term literary values than in the immediate news. Rheumatic or not, would these soldiers have to fight? Goaded thus, she regaled me in April, 1939, with another story, a charming one and right to the point:

"And listen, it is not because I do not want to answer about war, but you see 4, 3, 2, 5 years ago the [Paris] Herald called me up and asked me what I thought of the European war. I said I did not think there was going to be one although as I am mostly mistaken perhaps there was but I do not think so and I have been of the same mind ever since. I do not believe that there is one human being on the continent of Europe who wants a general European war, not even members of the armies and the navies of any European country and since they not one of them want a European war the chances are there will not be one, of course accidents can happen and chips on shoulders can be knocked off but when nobody wants a thing generally speaking if they have anything to do with it thèy avoid it, this conviction left me calm in September [Munich] and has left me calm ever since, did I tell you the wonderful thing one of the farmers of Bilignin said in September. He is a gentle soul but a good soldier 42 years old, and he was mobilized, I met him just before he went with his oxen and his wife and I said M. Lambert is there going to be war, no he said my wife is worried but no there will not be war, why not, I said, because said he parce que c'est pas logique, what does that mean I said, well he said, I am 42 years old and I fought the whole war, my son is 18 and he would fight this war and so would I, no he said it is not logical, if I were 60 and I had a grandson of 18, we would believe in war and a war might come, but I at 42 with a son of 18 no it is not logical, but said I that is alright for you but how about the germans and Italians, the same thing, he said, they talk differently but they feel the same. Well he went off and he came back and I met him with his oxen and his wife and I said, well M. Lambert there was no war. No he said no Mlle, c'etait pas logique. Well we may be all mistaken but there it is and it keeps us peaceful."

The Lambert incident was included in *Paris France*, which was published exactly a year later. In the book the men's ages are changed, or presumably corrected, and the wording is different. I do not know which was written first, but my original longhand account seems more effective than this following version, the first to be printed:

"Monsieur Lambert . . . is a tall thin man, a gentle soul, a good farmer and a good soldier, forty-five

186

years old. I met him with his wife and oxen. And I said you are leaving to go, Monsieur Lambert. Yes, he said, and my wife is crying. Is there going to be a war, I said. No, he said, my wife is crying but there is not going to be a war. Why not, I said. Because, said he, it is not logical. You see I am forty-five years old, I fought the whole of the last war, my son is seventeen years old, he and I would fight this war. It is not logical mademoiselle that I at forty-five who fought the war, with a son of seventeen, should believe in a general European war. It is not logical. Now said he, if I were sixty and my grandson was seventeen, we might both believe in a general European war and there might be a war, but I at forty-five and my son at seventeen, no Mademoiselle. It is not logical. But, I said, that is alright for you, the French are a logical people, but the Germans and the Italians. Mademoiselle, he said, they talk differently but they believe the same.

"Well he went away and then in almost ten days he came back and there he was on the road with his wife and his oxen, and I walking with my dogs met him. I said, Monsieur Lambert you were right there was no war. No he said no Mademoiselle it is not logical."

Hardly four months after I nagged Miss Stein into predicting there would be no war, Germany attacked Poland, and quite placidly, without any sign of rancor, she ate her words:

"Well here we are, I never did think there would be another war for me to see and here we are, well if there is one I would of course rather be in it than out of it, there is that something about a war."

Later, in *Wars I Have Seen*, she defined "that something": "I do not like to fish in troubled waters but I do like to see the troubled water and the fish and the fisherman."

Her letter continued: "We are for the present staying here [in Bilignin], we have done everything we can for everybody and they for us, we see Madame Pierlot often, she is bearing up pretty well as Rob does not go any more, he is past age . . . We have had a radio installed, I never listened to one before, there is a deplorable amount of music going on in the world, if they would suppress most of it perhaps the world would be more peaceful . . ."

She and Miss Toklas prepared at once to make the troubled waters stay away from their door: "Now did I tell you that we took a flying trip to Paris, and back and arranged about the pictures, and saw the world and are now back again in Bilignin, I do not know whether I did tell you, I have written so many letters these last few days, and I may drive the car for the butcheress or for the bakeress otherwise we are back to the daily life."

As a matter of fact, they had not managed to resume the "daily life" up to the time of Miss Stein's death, and after that Miss Toklas alone would never be able to attain it in the old sense. Even from the material point of view, Miss Toklas was still sharing, in 1947, the hardships which afflicted everyone else in Paris; she had too little heat, couldn't find shoes to buy, lacked butter, milk, poultry, fish, good bread, and she even hoarded bits of string . . . when packages from America arrive it always infuriates her to find some postal clerk has taken off the good stout imported twine and tied in its place the breakable native variety.

Nevertheless the two women, whose deaths seemed to me almost inevitable especially during the years when it was impossible to communicate with them, were unbelievably fortunate: they survived. They survived a brutal occupation to which thousands of other women succumbed in those terrible years, though constant deprivations must have shortened Miss Stein's life. They were not under fire, they did not freeze, they had a servant, the cupboard was never completely bare. At one critical period, after they lost contact with America, they found themselves literally penniless. A Frenchman, of whom Miss Toklas always speaks with heartfelt gratitude, lent them enough francs to meet expenses for six months, and refused to accept any security whatever; it was his interest in writing, and particularly in Miss Stein's, that inspired this kindness. Finally the expatriates sold the remaining Cézanne, a portrait of the artist's wife, and for the rest of the war "we ate Cézanne," they said, cannibal-fashion.

They occupied a special position, for unlike most Europeans they were entitled to a refuge in this country. The long journey would have been difficult but possible. While they worried about the high cost of living here, they could have managed; Miss Toklas would have learned to make both ends meet in America as well as France.

The truth was that they refused to desert in time of trouble the adopted land where they were so happy on days of fair weather. Having stuck it out in 1914–18, they would do it again. Already in their sixties, realizing they might be cut off from all their compatriots, in the possession of only meager resources, they stayed there loyally at the start when Hitler's strategy imposed upon the war a "phony" look and so made it seem less dangerous than in 1914, and still stayed after the quick defeat, when they had witnessed the struggle at about its bloodiest and might have felt impelled to flee.

I begged them to come, but even my redoubled efforts after 1939 failed to influence them. Offers of another lecture tour in the spring of 1940 raised my hopes and dashed them in a single sentence:

"We thought since there is nothing to do here xcept be peaceful we might do something for our Patrie over there, but the embassy tells me that it is easy to get over but would it be as easy to get back, and well we would not like it if we could not get back, so for the moment there or rather here we are."

After asking me to investigate the reliability of a bureau which had made her another lecturing proposition, Miss Stein was still troubled at the thought of deserting the French, and repeated: "Then also there seems the question of getting back." She touched once more on the subject: "There are two more agents who want me, but, of course there is the question of coming home again, for various reasons we could not stay away, in the first place we would go broke and the second place we would not want to."

The more I worried, the more cheerful and lively her letters became, despite periods of fearful uncertainty as when Hitler turned his panzers and dive-bombers westward in the spring of 1940: "I know you are having fits just now about us but, as yet nothing is happening hereabout which does not always happen."

As it had looked like a phony war, this could be a phony quiet, a respite before the full fury of the conflict swept into the mountainous department of the Ain. The flames spreading over all the rest of Europe were bound to blaze across Bilignin eventually, or so it seemed to me on this safe side of the Atlantic, and so it seemed in some dreadful moments to Miss Stein, for she confessed:

"I write to you quite often because I know you want to hear, we go along very peacefully and then sometimes about 10 o'clock in the evening I get scared about everything and then I complete[ly] upset Alice and she goes to bed scared and I walk in the garden and I come in and I work and I am all peaceful and luckily Alice can sleep and that is the worst moment, during the day we are busy and that is the way that is."

Since Miss Toklas and Miss Stein loved France from the bottom of their hearts, they asked no more of a chance than their servant Madame Roux, or their neighbors in Belley, Bilignin and Culoz. Perhaps the renunciation of an American refuge was unwise, but in these two lonely and helpless women it was brave. They were of a suspect and martyred race, and a mistrusted nationality in 1939, an enemy nationality in 1941; the nearest official help they could count on was from the U.S. consul in Lyon, who repeatedly advised them to go on home. They would not budge.

As the waves of the conflict rolled toward them, receded and again advanced, I realized that, even if they didn't start for their native land, there might be safer places in France than Bilignin, and of course they lived within a short auto ride of neutral, but expensive, Switzerland. One day I hoped they had headed east, next I hoped it was south, but it was obviously a quandary that they themselves, unable to guess which way the enemy would jump, couldn't solve. Miss Stein replied to one of my letters:

"I love your sentence, wondering whether we could endure staying here or the exact opposite, whether we could endure not staying here well you know the answer bless you." The answer was, they stayed.

With the belated entry of Italy into the war just before the French collapse in June, 1940, the situation changed drastically, and what I had longed for now scared me stiff, for if they were running away, they might run right into the arms of the new foe. Miss Stein answered:

"That was a wonderful sentence you wrote if then instead of moving as we've hoped you'd do, you'll stay where you were which is what we'll begin to hope from now on. That does tell that sentence of yours all our adventures and here we are we never did move . . . The worst days we kept saying to each other, golly the Kiddies must be worried about us and knowing the Kiddies were worrying like that was a great comfort, got your telegram alright but as yet we cannot telegraph or write by avion."

The surrender by Pétain replaced my immediate fears with anxiety over the possible, indeed the probable effects of Hitler's racial policies. But the cessation of Franco-German hostilities seemed to end about all the worries of Miss Stein and Miss Toklas. Airmail became available. . . . The women went to Lyon to have their passports "made beautiful and neutral at the American consulate" . . . There were vines to pull and trim, garden to hoe . . . Miss Toklas needed cigarettes . . . Pépé had fleas.

"Mrs. Roux and I cutting down trees well not big trees but still trees," Miss Stein wrote. "You can get wood but all the men are so busy with the récolte [harvest] as everybody has to do the work of two or three, as they have to do the work for the women whose men are gone as well as their own that we have undertaken to saw our wood and now we are both so keen on it that it is hard to get hold of the saw. I had no idea that the technique of wood sawing was so easy to acquire."

Later she claimed: "I love to saw wood, and your [flash] light that you gave us is so useful we are all carrying them in our pockets when we walk and I saw wood by it."

Benefiting by the hard experiences of the 1939–40 winter, they managed to keep comfortably warm: "To be sure we have not had any coal but in this country of wood coal really is not at all necessary, wood heats so much warmer than coal if you have lots of it, and we have big oak logs and small acacia branches for the dining room and the kitchen stove and I saw it and it burns and all has gone so very well."

They fished for fish and exercise, they went nutting and mushrooming, they gleaned in the fields for salad greens, dug dahlias, walked the dogs, drove, talked. Madame Roux played "Rebecca at the well," and life assumed a "Biblical" cast. Miss Toklas read cookbooks, her favorite, and garden books. Miss Stein's literary fare, heterogeneous in peacetime by preference, was the same now by necessity: *Uncle Tom's Cabin, The Vicar of Wakefield, Swiss Family Robinson, War and Peace,* mystery and detective stories, Dickens, Ouida, Mrs. Oliphant, Prescott, Byron and Shakespeare, and she asked me for a list of volumes which included Howells' *A Hazard of New Fortune* as good wartime reading. And as if I didn't think she was keeping busy, here was a schedule:

"I am writing an extra letter too, it is snowing all day, and I have cut wood all day and read War and Peace of Tolstoy's all day."

She also wanted dental floss and darning cotton: "There is one thing though and that Mildred can help Alice, and that is white darning thread, there is no more and could you put a few yards in every letter because towels and napkins have to be mended, darned, and there is no more darning cotton, so take a few yards loose and put it in a letter and so Alice can go on darning the family linen."

Stockings, for example, were darned until they were practically all darn and no stocking; Miss Toklas worked on them up to fifty separate darns and after that, she decided, she and Miss Stein could go barefoot.

Miss Stein renewed the request: "But do keep on with the darning cotton, because you cannot buy new sheets towels etc, and so Alice mends and mends and

194

that takes a lot of darning thread, every time she gets some of yours she shouts with joy and relief, do not worry about us, we just have each had a suit of clothes made by a Molyneux tailor who is refuged in the neighborhood, so we are most chic and warm."

For a time we sprinkled soap flakes in every letter: "Another soapy envelope came and it smells deliciously soapy, ivory soap it floats, thanks and thanks again, our neighbor half Mexican half English and very charming, was here when it came, how says she it does smell of the American continent."

There was also "a flower [soapwort] that grows that is particularly useful as soap, and it grows here, and besides we did have a fair supply of toilet soap, so our daily bath is not only refreshing but cleansing, and the most difficult thing to hold out in is stockings and cigarettes and kitchen towels, but alas xcept for mending the two and doing without the third seems to be the only thing we can do, we are quite happy with wooden soles to our shoes, in fact in cold weather they keep you warm and you don't slip in the snow."

Finally: "Soaping has been gotten the better of, we can take our daily bath and hair-wash, it is alright, and Mme Roux washes in wood ashes that is the clothes and so that is all comfortable now." Wood ash "makes clothes much sweeter and cleaner than soap, you tie up wood ashes in a cloth and you boil it with the wash, they always used to and now they do again, to wash ourselves we have plenty of soap, so do not worry, we are if anything cleaner than we were." . . . And that was very clean, I remembered, for Miss Stein used to like fresh sheets every night, and she herself always had a fresh-air, tweedy smell.

While my fears for their safety had quieted, I now wondered how they could possibly get along, keep warm in winter, stay well fed, cure a cold. They were approaching the age when many women in peaceable countries require special foods and medicines, are careful not to wet their feet, and spend long hours beside a fire.

The merciful truth was, that they were allowed a sort of training period. War closed in bit by bit. Hardship was cumulative rather than instantaneous, so that in the course of five years they moved from plenty down through one substitute and makeshift after another almost but never quite to destitution. They began, for instance, with a car and the gasoline to run it; lost the gas and so the use of the car; received a special gas permit; like everybody else were obliged to change from gas to alcohol; could buy no more alcohol but lent the car to a friend who could; finally were reduced to shanks' mare.

The auto was not equipped with a heater anyway, though they drove it in the icy shadows of the Alps. But it was an extraordinary convenience and they rejoiced at the formal grant of the right to purchase fuel "in recognition of what I have written about France and that makes that so much easier . . . and the first thing we did was to take Mme Pierlot to Chambery and we crossed the Rhone on a flat boat and saw the busted bridges and some of the bombarded houses and it is all very strange and very real . . ."

196

The "gazogène," as they called the alcohol-burner, was "just like the good old last war's Ford, you coax and you shove, and you add mixture, and you tug in the moving and you hold your breath up hill, it's most xciting and remindful." When worse came to worst they were not discouraged: "There is always a replacement, we are all in the era of barter, le troc as they all say here now, nobody wants money they want goods, and it is all most xciting."

They helped to run a "Foyer du Soldat," according to a letter bearing the not very clear rubber-stamp heading:

FOYER DU SOLDAT
Bilignin par Belley (Ain)

Miss Stein explained: "There you are the first one to have our stamp. The foyer [the French YMCA] is not all ready yet but the stamp is, but it is getting ready. Did I tell you about it, we are making a sport center in the barn, and another foyer in the little salle [hall] near the four communale [community oven], we are very busy, just as busy as we can be, anybody who wants to send us a foot-ball or anything else will be gratefully" [that's the word with which she finished].

She adjusted herself philosophically to this hardy and precarious existence: "Just at present we are all very quiet waiting for what comes next, but there is one thing one has learnt and that is to empty your mind of all thinking about things you cannot manage, in fact you kind of learn not to think and not to plan but like the busy bee to be very busy, and to busy yourself with that."

She discovered a new writer, a poet who lived in her neighborhood. She kept in touch by telephone with the artist Balthus and other friends beyond the range of the car. The Red Cross visited her:

"The American Red Cross is coming to see us this week, and that will be a touch from home, don't know whether there will be any other kind of touch, here's hoping."

Therese Bonney, on a mission for the Library of Congress, dropped in to photograph them and the village and "then they came back again night before last at 8.30 and stayed till one o'clock in the morning in the pleasant American way and then left for Lyon, we all talked and it was wonderful, it was like as if there was no war and never had been one, perhaps there isn't anyway."

She heard that Thornton Wilder was in Intelligence service, and asked what had become of Ernest Hemingway. She drove to Lyon to attend a lecture by Bernard Faÿ. She wrote.

She balanced unsteadily between "very cheerful too cheerful and then not cheerful at all." She had her ups in good weather, her downs in bad, felt grand when mail arrived and miserable when it did not . . . "Sometimes I even get so perplexed I think we will go to Bordeaux but that passes like other things." And after Pearl Harbor: "When I write now I wonder if you will get it . . . now we do not know how you are and where you are, and what you are doing and feeling, it is the first time since the debacle that you seem far away and we hope every day that a letter will come from you and then that they will keep coming . . . We think of you all as you all thought of us, only we think of you doubly because after all us is us."

In the midst of everything, as if they didn't have enough problems to cope with, they were evicted. It was the second time they'd been forced out of a home in which, it seemed to me, they were very happy, but for the second time Miss Stein in her optimistic way made the best of it. When they had to move from the rue de Fleurus, she wrote me: "Alice and I had been talking about that [the possibility of moving] . . . no servant would stand the kitchen, there was no air in the house, the garage they had built next door had made it very uncomfortable," and so she pretended to be glad to leave.

When they were ousted from Bilignin: "We were in despair and now we have found a place on the other side of the valley that we liked even better." However, there were reasons other than the nature of their new and larger quarters in Culoz, nearer the château de Béon, for liking it. As a railroad town, this location was more important than Bilignin to the Germans, whose hand lay less onerously on the population which supplied labor to keep essential trains running. That advantage accrued to them by chance. Another boon of inestimable value was the complaisance of the local French government in the matter of registration; a German regulation requiring their names in the village files was winked at by friendly officials, and it is impossible to guess what they were spared by not appearing on any lists subject to enemy scrutiny. Although they were known to the invaders, for a colonel or two and more than a hundred soldiers were quartered on them at various times, they seem not to have been identified.

Instead of famine, there was an occasional feast. For their first wartime Thanksgiving they planned a "real" dinner with turkey, near mince meat, Hubbard squash, "but alas no sweet potatoes or Kiddie Korn," and though it was an early winter, the grapes were all in, "and a lovely crop they were, but the apples are all wormy this year which is sad and there are no nuts but almonds, they too were wormy and we think of American nut stores with tender longing."

After France's defeat Miss Stein replied to anxious inquiries:

"So far the food business has not been bad and is not likely to be here in this country, which produces enough for us but not enough to send away what with the difficulties of transport, so everything [meaning everybody] about thinks we will be alright here, it is the big cities that suffer, I walk in and out of Belley every other day, and then our little maid goes in on her bicycle and gathers up what I have bought, and once a week Alice walks in and gives it all the once over."

In a later letter: "Belley has been full of xcitement, the butchers and the charcutiers [delicatessen store proprietors] went on strike, said they could not make enough money and refused to give us meat and they were all put into the local gaol and it all has been most xciting we were front page news even in Lyon and

Grenoble for almost three days and Belley did not know whether to be proud or ashamed, do not worry about us, we get along very nicely with the food ration, fortunately the hunting season is open and there seems to be plenty of game and that helps out a lot and what with chickens and rabbits and liver for the dogs which are not on [ration] cards, there is no privation, there is plenty of bread and one way and another plenty of fat . . ."

More details followed: "We did miss sugar but now they have discovered how to make sugar out of grapes and there is plenty of that and it makes nice deserts you get a liquid kind and a solid kind and the other day we got a white kind of the consistency of solid honey made of white raisins and the most heavenly flavor and Alice made a layercake of it and it was the most delicious food, and so it goes on, just when it seems all over then something else turns up which is the french way . . ." Miss Toklas is accorded the proper credit: "As Alice does know how to make everything be something we get along fine."

In the spring of 1941, "It rains all the time and the garden turns yellow instead of green, and the potatoes grow too high and do not flower, all these things these days are of capital importance, but then as I remember it was like this last year and we had lots all the same."

Her optimism was not very reassuring, because I suspected then as I was to learn for certain eventually, that when it came to hardships she invariably painted the picture in the brightest colors; if it wasn't good news, it wasn't news and I didn't hear about it at all. But in this case the crop prospects were not overestimated, apparently, for at the last Thanksgiving before the United States entered the war, she wrote:

"We have just had our neighbors [for dinner] that is they helped with supplies and we ate it here a real Thanksgiving dinner. You know I told you that we have neighbors a nice frenchman married to a half Scotch half Spanish Mexican, and they have turkeys, and cows, etc. so they supplied the turkey butter and cream and this was the menu, A cream celery soup, a gratin made of Hubbard squash, our garden, a turkey with chestnut stuffing, mashed potatoes, vegetable salad, mince pie and ice cream, not so bad and we all ate lots . . . and Alice cooked it wonderfully and the frenchman said it was not Alice in Wonderland but Wonderland chez Alice [at Alice's], as I say when you live on restrictions a big blow out once in a while digests as sweetly as possible. You do get rid of lots of indigestion dining on restrictions in the country, in the cities not so good, not so bad for adults but not so good for the young, well anyway I knew you would be pleased to know we ate . . ."

Weather was important not only because it affected the crops but also because it could change Miss Stein's mood from gay to sad and back again. She delighted in "pearly" October mornings; the "gentle white" of winter, the first cuckoos and swallows of spring, but she also wrote:

"The winter at least January February and March until now when it is over were long and cold and moist and covered with dirty snow, that never was removed and never went away, but now the sun is shining everybody is digging or hunting for salads in the fields . . ."

By fall the note was wholly cheerful: "We are now wondering whether we should get a goat because the pasturage has gone bad and a goat can eat anything, and I might take it out on winter days and have it eat snow, I suppose even a goat would draw the line at that, the feeding proposition in France has its ups and downs of course it was not nice of it not to rain, but anyhow we have had two hares hunting has commenced, and so the daily life goes on . . ." Shortly afterward: "We are busy getting our Winter vegetables into the cellar, we have been eating lots of game."

They imitated their neighbors in adopting what the French called the système D, D standing for se débrouiller, to straighten things out, to muddle through. Their hit-or-miss existence could be the death of them at any minute, but there was never a hint of despair, and though they ought to have been on the point of tears, they always saw the funny and the sunny side, and reported on it. As Miss Stein had preferred a lively human anecdote to a discussion of the possibility of war, so now she preferred a good story to any serious consideration of the likelihood of starvation. The d'Aiguys, for instance, scouring the fields for food, made a mistake:

"The Beon family ate rhubarb leaves as salad and they are feeling kind of funny."

In the cold winter of 1940 when dogs as well as humans suffered, shivery Pépé, who did not survive the war, needed special attention:

"Golly it's cold, it does not feel as if we were on the Southern side of the Massif Centrale but we are, the sun

203

shines and says we are but Alice and Pepe and our little servant who just went into Belley and back on her bicycle says definitely we are not. Basket and I incline to believe we are. Pepe has just had himself made a beautiful military coat by a military tailoress in Belley and does look most awfully swagger, with a high starchy collar. He says now everybody admires him and pays no attention to Basket which is a pleasure."

While it must have exhausted the two women's ingenuity to feed these pets, they proved to be an inexhaustible comfort, and Mrs. Kiddie and I paid them much attention in our letters, to one of which Miss Stein replied:

"One of the darkest days and there have been quite a few of them well or ones of them Mrs. Kiddies' letter to Basket II came along and cheered us up, it may not have cheered Basket but it certainly did us . . . Alice and Mrs. Roux they are just full of pep so is Pepe . . . The Christmas letters and cards have all come but not Basket's gift but we still hope, not Basket he in the simple spirit of a village dog is busy with dogs and sticks, and not a passionate eater but a very sweet village dog and very handsome . . . The book for Christmas for Basket has come and I cannot say that he has said anything about it, but we liked it, Basket is a sweet dog but he has only two ideas, one is to jump very high with all four feet in the air and the other is to run around with a stick in his mouth, he is not a conversational dog but Pepe is conversational enough for six, but anyway Basket is grateful, he would prefer a cookie but not so us and he is grateful."

204

Miss Stein grouped the dogs with goats, chickens, casual acquaintances and the home as the "society" she decided she preferred, and ruled out cats, cows, rabbits, gardens, trees and hills.

Even during the worst years she was not lonely: "So far our trouble has been rather too much society rather than too little." If she liked Bilignin and Culoz, the townspeople liked her and Miss Toklas, too; popular in peacetime, they earned the honest admiration of their neighbors for deliberately casting in their lot with them during the war. The expatriates entered into community activities, helped with aid for veterans, assisted in an art show. In the spring of 1942 Miss Stein wrote:

"We are going to have a real salon de peinture in Belley, there are about 15 painters refugees and local here and they are going to have a salon and a vernissage just like Paris we are all awfully xcited, it will last from the 1–15 of May."

Then came more information: "We are most xcited about our salon for the artistes du Bugey, it really is beginning to look quite handsome of course it is helped by strangers who live in our midst, I am chief of the hanging committee and I spend every afternoon at Belley saying a little higher a little lower now a little to the right and to the left, as I am the only member of the committee who does not paint naturally my word is law and it all is very xciting, we even have two large pieces of sculpture done by a Russian lady who is somewhere around and has xhibited at all salons and we have one Belley lady who says she is hors concours and so has to have the best place, and then there is a tambola each xhibitor has to give one picture, some do not want to give one and some want to give seven, but I remain firm, then our kind friends and neighbors who have a wood burning automobile as he has a textile factory took us over to Grenoble and there we saw the museum . . . xtraordinary how many people paint in France, and paint well, all ages, I suppose we should not be astonished but I am a little . . ."

The *Petit Dauphinois,* using a photograph of "personnalités belleysannes" at the opening, with Miss Stein among them, offered profuse congratulations to the three natives who originated the idea, and continued:

"Happy trio who had the inestimable good fortune to talk of their project to Mme Gertrude Stein who is perhaps the one woman in the world best informed about painting and its history, great painting as well as ordinary . . ." Maybe Miss Stein took this with a grain of salt, as Miss Toklas takes with several grains the "vous qui savez tout" [you who know everything] with which Madame Picasso nowadays prefaces questions to her; but I'm not convinced the Dauphinois, or Madame Picasso either, exaggerates very much.

The art show led to an academy: "Imagine as the result of the show in Belley they have started an academy . . . the very young and the very old artists draw and are criticized by a Russian sculptress who is a daughter of an ancien [former] director of her country's Beaux Arts, they even had an Italian model nude to his waist, great xcitement, there is a perfect passion for art these days in Belley."

Perhaps the best parts of the wartime letters concerned fellow villagers, whom Miss Stein met and with whom she gossiped frequently in the course of her long walks. Just as hostilities started, she reported:

"We had two alerts, the pays [region] has two schools of thought about that, Mme. Vautherie says that here among the mountains, so many mountains inevitably they will lose themselves and not get here, why they should get here nobody seems to know and Mme Chanel says that when airplanes fly they are bound to arrive ici et la [here and there], but then Mme Chanel is cynical, she says that her son-in law is not far away although mobilized and goes to see his wife on his bicycle from time to time, and I said alors il lui donne un coup de main, plus tot un coup d'oeil says she. [The comeback sounds smarter in French than English: "Then he gets some work done for her, rather he gets a good look at her."] She also adds that men are naturally crazy, they are ready to fight just because it rains too much, but that is normal craziness, when it gets abnormal like the Germans well then you have to do something about it, after all the french are, says she, fully free and [Miss Stein's comment] en effet [in fact] they are."

She had warm praise for her neighbors: "I must say though it was rather wonderful the way every person in the village at the news of the invasion of Belgium before they thought of their own troubles said ces pauvres gens le deuxieme fois envahi, Ces pauvres gens [those poor people, invaded a second time, those poor people], of course we have alertes and naturally everybody is troubled about somebody, but otherwise you know how it is, life goes on . . . So now you can't say that I did not mention the war, but of course naturally it is not natural to talk about it."

After America became a belligerent, Miss Stein and Miss Toklas became allies as well as friends of the French. Regarded previously with amicable respect, they all of a sudden symbolized the community's saviors, and in a way victory came to be expected personally of them; they changed from guests to protectors. That made everybody happier, without making things easier for Miss Stein, who explained:

"At present we are most busy being Americans, everybody has so much faith in us, as we are their only hope and they do believe, and we do get worried lest we might fail them but I do not think we will, but so much faith does frighten one a bit, Bob d'Aiguy has always had it and when the other day he said that when he hears over the wire [radio] every day the Star Spangled Banner, he has tears in his eyes, it all brings back the days of the Kiddie they all feel just like that, well we did it then and we will do it again."

There are two characteristic stories about Madame Pierlot. She couldn't "tell the difference whether it is her grandfather and her father and their friends talking about '70 or her sons and their friends talking about '40." And then: "Mme Pierlot was telling me that Bob had found an old book of her grandfathers Caesar's commentaries and he read it aloud to them and he said mother the French nor the Germans have changed since Caesar's day, it is all true, and added Mme Pierlot, my Grandfather read it aloud to my mother and myself in 1870 and he made exactly the same remark."

"We felt pretty shocked about it," Miss Stein said of Pearl Harbor, "sort of could not get over it until I began to say in a refrain, they will solemnly go to and fro and every day they will solemnly bomb Tokio, and I began to feel better . . ."

This strange, perhaps absurd incantation is not just another bit of Steiniana, a passage out of a new *Tender Buttons* or *Four Saints*. It's the sort of magic rigmarole by which children, and primitive or harried or desperate peoples, lay ghosts. Though it may sound crazy to an American, many Frenchmen in that trying day would have repeated it gladly in the hope it might work, in the sorry realization that if it didn't, there was precious little else they could do about it. Mumbo-jumbo was better than nothing.

In their feverish need for some reassurance, the citizens of Belley and Bilignin easily surpassed this, however, and recalled some prophecies and forecasts by saints long dead, and read into them promises of deliverance. Miss Stein, sternly realistic in most matters and as cynical as any latter-day scientist about the occult, was at one with her neighbors in this. "I always rightfully believe and believed in every superstition," she had said in *Everybody's Autobiography*. If she shared Frenchmen's hardships, she would not be denied their solace. Jeanne d'Arc had only heard voices; the men and women of the beleaguered Bugey with their own eyes saw it in black and white. Saints arose from the misty past, described the manifold miseries of the 1940's and foretold their end. Beginning shortly after the fall of France, Miss Stein wrote frequently about it:

"Everybody is feeling more hopeful and the prophecies go on, we are all now completely devoted to St. Odile, who says the germans will leave France being impelled thereto by a mal etrange [peculiar sickness], and I am not sure that she is not right, the best ones are St. Odile and the 1680 are of le moine [monk] Johannes, some day we will send you a copy of that."

Later: "I have come across lots of new old predictions since [the last time they were mentioned in these letters], everybody brings them to me and tells me about them and I like it, and as they all predict the same, not too long away and France victor and it is a comfort."

According to the "Prédictions de Saint Godefroy en 1853," from *Le Moniteur* of April of that year, at the start of the ninth month of 1939 Germany would be attacked by the Francs and Anglo-Saxons; about the middle of 1940 the Germans aided by the Latins would capture Paris, the Francs would cease fighting, Rome would burn, the Latins would be defeated in the deserts of Egypt, the Anglo-Saxons would take over Germany in 1941 and royalty would be restored in France bringing peace and prosperity.

The cult of Godefroy began after the events which corroborated in part his long forgotten forecast. Since time proved him partly right, it should perhaps be added here for those in whom he inspires confidence, that he prophesied "a sort of revolution" for 1948 and believed that, beginning in 1980, "the era of anti-Christ is foreseen for sixty years."

In August, 1941, when there was little alcohol for Miss Stein's car: "Looks as if there was not going to be any more but Saint Odile says October and so far she had never been anything but right and we believe . . ." Soon afterward: "Everybody is feeling much encouragement and Saint Odile is full of hope for October." When October arrived with little to justify faith in Saint Odile, or Saint Two, Saint Ten, or however many saints are there in it, Miss Stein assured me: "St. Odile is still going strong."

Needing more desperately to encourage them than they ever needed encouragement, I donned the prophet's robe and wrote enigmatically that things were coming along fine and some day, at a date set prudently a full year away, their dearest hopes would be fulfilled. I received the reply:

"I read [to the American consul and Madame d'Aiguy] how you said that this time next year the good news would be so big that there would be no type big enough and we were all pleased," and Miss Stein added: "We believe in St. Kiddy and everything he tells."

In November, 1942, the prophecies began to pay off. When the Americans landed in Africa, Miss Stein noted jubilantly: "The kiddies the new kiddies are coming nearer and nearer . . . I have stated your predictions to everybody about the good news in the fall and nothing but good news and they believe in you next only to Saint Odile and more even more."

If it is tragic, as legend teaches us, to be a prophet and not to be believed, it is at the least embarrassing not

211

to be a prophet and to be believed, and so, reluctant to compete with Odile, Godefroy and Johannes, I quit trying to brighten up tomorrow.

4

The *Bugiste*, local weekly, was loyally interested in local matters, and its editor interviewed Miss Stein. To the question, "How do you write," she replied, said the paper without quoting her: "Walking, talking, bathing, reading, sleeping. On little scraps of time and paper. In fragments strictly illegible. In a Harlequin outfit . . ."

Though at the moment she was working on a novel which she called *Mrs. Reynolds* and to which she referred once or twice, I trust mistakenly, as *Mrs. Rogers*, the *Bugiste* reported:

"And nevertheless it's about another [book] that she talks. How stimulated, and how inexhaustible, she is about another one, of immediate news value: the Franco-American Committee has asked her to translate for her compatriots Marshal Pétain's messages. M. Gabriel-Louis Jaray has made all the arrangements with her. It wasn't easy to find the English equivalent for the 'brevitas imperatoria' but this rivalry between the two languages stirs her; now she feels she's going to win, she abandons herself to her subject, to her hero, she admires the importance of his words and the significance of the symbol.

"She binds the texts together with short notes: There, his prophetic manner of conceiving history triumphs; she has already finished the introduction, the most perfect example of the method by which, speaking a child's language, she finds, as the child does, the means of making the most fragile truths understood by the great people of her country and others, without shocking anyone. It will be an event, this presentation of the France of today to America."

Though the project doesn't seem today very momentous, at the time it promised, or rather threatened, to be an event in several ways, and I doubted whether it could be done "without shocking anyone." When she described her enthusiasm, I wrote at once that, if she'd forgive my pointing it out, it would appear to me unwise to assume the role of Marshal's advocate in this country. Other considerations aside, conservative literary elements would not be persuaded to an interest in her own writing by her defense of Pétain's, and liberals might be so offended as to reject her works.

That did not faze her in the least: "The translating of the Marshal's speeches is a fascinating occupation, I don't suppose the Atlantic Monthly would care to do my introduction which is good and I am going to do an epilogue, but I will write you more and more about all that."

Her notion that the *Atlantic* might be interested may have been incorrect but was understandable, for that was the magazine which, though now under different editorship, had published Ellery Sedgwick's article praising some aspects of Franco's Spain. It was none of my business, but I felt a personal obligation to make it clear that I disagreed, and if that were to mean that "when the flowers of friendship faded friendship faded,"

I would have been forced, disturbing though the prospect was, to submit.

America, watching with increasing consternation as two French military heroes retreated before Hitler's armies, was dumbfounded when the third, the almost legendary World War I chieftain, surrendered. He could have carried on from Africa, he should have displayed the fortitude of a Churchill, he still commanded a great fleet, it was protested. And with this disappointment, his critics recalled damagingly the reactionary aspects of his career, such as his admiration for Franco and, above all, the servility of Vichy.

An opposite point of view was held by the United States Department of State, apparently, and by other people. Pétain ostensibly had fenced off a part of his land from which the conquerors were barred; if he hadn't used the fleet, he still hadn't lost it; he had preserved Paris; temporarily he had spared many Frenchmen from the horrors suffered for instance by Norwegians.

Undoubtedly the official United States attitude toward him colored the attitude of his subjects, as he seemed to regard them, in unoccupied France. It cannot be denied that, in defending him, Miss Stein spoke not only for herself but for many Frenchmen who at least in 1940 and 1941 believed, like our own government and with even more supposed reasons for it, that he had done his best for his country. Nothing came of the proposed translation, and since Miss Stein had undertaken it at a time and in a place where complete information was not available, it might be dismissed by itself as an unfortunate error in judgment.

214

But even with the perspective which postwar years allowed, even when she learned how unpopular Pétain was, she remembered gratefully the benefits he seemed to have secured for France and, in *Wars I Have Seen* (1945) she recorded her persistent approval of his refusal to continue the struggle from African bases, and of his negotiation of an armistice with the Germans. While she "did not like his way of saying I Philippe Petain," still "we were in the unoccupied area and that was a comfort. Many months later somebody wrote to me and said that in America everybody said there was no difference between the occupied and unoccupied zone but we who lived in the unoccupied zone we knew there was a difference all right."

I was "somebody" and "everybody" was a young man newly returned from warring Europe with an account he had given me of the situation there. Miss Stein had answered my letter more sharply in private than in the book: "And your young man was badly informed, the difference between occupied and unoccupied is not technical but fundamental and don't you forget it."

Taken by itself, the Pétain incident is not conclusive proof of a conservative point of view; if I had believed that Pétain helped to save my neck, I too might seek to exculpate him from the more flagrant charges of collaboration.

This was not an isolated instance, however, and I was all the more alarmed as I remembered previous correspondence and conversations in which Miss Stein exhibited a reactionary position. I cannot recall verbatim

215

our many arguments about Spain in 1937, but several letters may and probably must be quoted.

While civil war raged beyond the Pyrenees, I protested to Miss Stein that people surely had the right to choose their own government, and in reply she wrote from Belley:

"I interested all our french friends here who are all Croix de feu [that is, potential supporters of Vichy] by telling them how you felt about Spain you see in Spain and to a certain xtent in France you cannot change the government when the people no longer want it, we ourselves had some such difficulty in the civil war, after all it does happen, and the Reds in Spain did not really any longer do what the people wanted beside after all here in France and I know a lot more about it than I did once anybody gets in power its hard to dislodge, like Tammany. You see in the old days the government changed all the time there were so many parties, but Stavisky was a real boss and he organized the Radical Socialists to stay and that machinery is still functioning though the real majority are tired of it, and as that majority are really there, or else the change of regime would not succeed as it does succeed, so you see you must not be too pedantic about the de facto government."

As I pressed her on the subject, she answered—and this was still three years before World War II threw a definitive light on the issues:

"About politics well about politics you see my dear kiddy I know I too believed in constitutional republican government but, look at it with the eye of the observer and not with the eye of the son of New England, the fact is that the only country that has really a constitutional government is England and in the first place she invented it and in the second place her population she being an island has not really enormously increased but when populations do increase majorities cease to be interesting, you know that well enough and in America . . . we limit the rule of the dictator but congress has been tending too strictly to be a yes congress, you know that, and disguise it to yourself as you will the majority does want a dictator, it is natural that a majority if it has come to be made up of enormous numbers do, a big mass likes to be shoved as a whole because it feels it moves and they cannot possibly feel that they move themselves as little masses can, there you are, like it or not there we are, and the latins being more logical than we know what they have not got and they know they have not got a constitutional government and so they get rid of it, of course they do not believe in majorities because in a latin country there is no such thing . . . [In Italy under Mussolini] they do let you work and live in the country and be peaceful . . . and really that is where they all are, they are all envious of Italy because everybody there can live and be quiet, and everybody xcept the few who make the noise want to live a little while and be quiet . . . and nobody thinks you can live and be quiet under communism, nor under constitutional government as made today, that is the impression of the workers who work and the peasants and the middle class . . ."

That was not the end of her lecture:

"You see what in Europe everybody is hollering about is whether communism is not worse than fascism

217

and here everybody thinks you have to be either red or white and I am not sure they are not right and certainly white is bad but not so bad as red. After all the people don't mean anything, there are about 5 in every European village that holler, sometimes the majority red and sometimes the majority white, and the remaining 10 are just scared and say yes to whatever they think is the stronger, now you cannot call that a government by the people, I must say my sympathy is largely with the 10 who are scared, it would be nice if they could be let alone but can they, I can be scared myself so I know how they feel. Down in Belley when they were all hollering one old duck was listening to gauche and droite [left and right] and finally he said well anyway one does always keep ones pocket book in one's right hand pocket. The relation of government to art is funny, Russia as they [critic Waldemar Georges, sculptor Jacques Lipschitz and others] were saying will stand for nothing but the most Bourgeois painting, they want nothing advanced at all, they are all for bourgeoisie in art, Lipschitz was in tears, he said it was wonderful in Russia but why were they so middle class in art, Hitler does not want any art at all, and Mussolini wants anything that helps Italian manufacture, and art does, and France well as I was saying to Bernard Faÿ it is to be remarked that under monarchy and empire all the great writers of France were in the academy but since the xistence of the 3rd republic not one, so as my grandfather used to remark there is a great deal to be said on both sides. As to their not letting me write, well most of them do let you write and I guess it would have taken me just about as long to be published anywhere as anywhere. I have been thinking about what you said about my writing and the social question. Not quite that. When I gave the lecture to the french students they too asked me about proletarian literature and I said one of my troubles was that for me gens [people] were just gens, and really they arouse a different kind of interest if you like one class or another class, like dull or not dull but really otherwise they were just what they were that is people. Every class has a kind of charm and since occupations and distribution and force and brains and personality are bound to be different inevitably there are bound to be classes and each class undoubtedly is what it is and the members of it have that kind of charm. Even the small bourgeoisie has its charm, at different moments of the world's history they make a fetish of one class's charm as against another, but to me they all have charm and aside from the class distinction which is inevitable they are all just themselves which is to me interesting. It is the story I tried to tell in the Making of Americans, and I would be interested in you writing something about it."

This may be the place to act on her suggestion. *The Making of Americans* concerns a bourgeois family whose intellectual interests, if any, are ignored while its members are being reduced to the terms of a lowest common denominator, which is, to a proletarian level. They eat, sleep, breathe, occupy houses, see one another, react in an unmechanical way to the mechanics of living. They are universal; indeed, it was Miss Stein's objective not

219

to create the individual but the mass, to "finally describe really describe every kind of human being there ever was or is or would be living."

The earlier *Three Lives*, already identified as proletarian literature by professed proletarians, is accepted without question as one of our most moving and original humanitarian documents. No liberal can complain about the early Stein. A canny conservative society should have burned her and her first two novels at the stake, but perhaps it schemed to serve its purposes better by preserving and converting her. When it became interested in her, and bought as well as praised her work, it would have been only natural for her in return to accept its ideas with less and less challenge. That sort of protective coloration fades red out to pink and pink out to white, "which is not so bad as red." It could have been, though of course unconsciously, tit for tat.

Miss Stein was born into a bourgeois background, and was a Republican all her life. The wonder is that she was such a rebel in art and creative writing, where she won her unique reputation, not that she was so conservative in the unfamiliar fields of economics and politics. She was a rentier, and possessed a rentier mentality in matters of taxes, jobs and government. It's a common habit to ascribe all the virtues to any person distinguished for the possession of one of them. In Miss Stein's case this is a serious fallacy. Without her fixed income we might never have heard of the rue de Fleurus, but with it we should not be surprised to find her disapproving of Roosevelt and the New Deal, believing in rugged individualism, favoring a gold basis for the dollar, regarding a man out of work as lazy or incompetent, thinking every American always could take care of himself, and advising GI's to fend bravely for themselves instead of looking to the community for a chance to make a livelihood.

In economic matters she was always conservative, but in politics she went from conservative to more conservative. The path to success was not necessarily straight ahead, but sidewise, from left to right. If her writing alone does not substantiate this, the circles of her friends do; they were liberal, or at least open-minded painters and writers at the start but they became Croix de Feu members or the Duchess of This or Count So-and-So.

As Miss Stein remarked, we learn to know people bit by bit, and there is always the possibility that what I define here as a movement away from liberal may be merely a movement within me; perhaps what I regard as change in her is no more than the gradual revelation of her attitudes to me. But I think I am right in locating the progression itself in Miss Stein.

It developed, or was disclosed to me, during the depression of the Thirties, when economic pressures drove many people to extreme positions. Half of it persisted after the war, when she retained her inalterable disapproval of the New Deal and all it represented. It appeared also to persist in politics for, as already noted, she defended Pétain and she also remained the firm friend of Bernard Faÿ, who after her death was imprisoned on collaborationist charges. Miss Stein would have denied them; in his way he was a loyal Frenchman who, appointed head of the Bibliothèque Nationale during the

German occupation, had accepted the post not to curry favor with his country's enemy but to preserve his country's treasures . . . and the fact is, not a volume was removed from that venerable institution. But here again, the issue is complicated; if he had indeed been known to Miss Stein as a collaborationist, she still would have been justified, many would think, in aiding him as the translator of some of her books, an intimate friend of many years and a frequent guest.

At least one critic accused her of revealing some sympathy for Fascism in *Wars I Have Seen*. He was almost ten years too late. When political issues were clarified by the eventual line-up of powers in the second World War, it was as plain to Miss Stein as it was to all the rest of us that there were no two ways about it, it had to be democracy, it couldn't be totalitarianism. After 1940 and 1941 she never would have written the already cited letter: "About politics you see my dear kiddy . . ." As hard facts had changed her mind about the possibility of war, they now settled her doubts about government . . . it was in another connection that she wrote, in *Operas and Plays*, that "I find I have changed my meaning in changing my meaning from the meaning I had to this meaning." Given the occasion, she would have been equally quick to acknowledge her new point of view, for when she held an opinion, whether it was shared or challenged by the whole world, she was entirely frank about it. It didn't matter whether she and I agreed, as she once wrote me; it didn't matter to her whether she and anybody agreed. With a little more reticence, or as I prefer to say, with a shred less honesty, she would never have been confronted with these unsavory accusations. In her day the woods were full of Fascist-minded writers prudent enough to keep their mouths shut; there are plenty of them around now. When all the facts became available to them, they did not change their minds. Miss Stein did. Her record in her last years was faultless. In *Wars I Have Seen*, she wrote:

"The fashion is the fashion, and republics simply republican republics are going to be the fashion."

In a letter there was a more homely expression of it one wartime spring when she was planting my corn in her garden: "And it is allied corn you can be sure."

After all, she lived in the midst of the maquis, who gave short shrift to collaborators or even suspected sympathizers. Many of the closing pages of her book are devoted to praise of their bravery and effectiveness. Fighters in the Resistance, hiding in the mountains around the village of Culoz, were her neighbors and friends; they knew where she stood, and it was exactly where they wanted her. "Honneur aux maquis" that saved Paris, she exclaimed. Her play, *Yes Is for a Very Young Man*, is the dramatic expression of unimpeachable democratic ideals; the very history of it corroborates its content, for she objected to an army production that was to be for the benefit of officers rather than soldiers.

Even if her position still seems dubious to some, she will be remembered inevitably for her novels, not her politics, just as her close friend Picasso will be remembered for his painting and not his ardent adoption of the Leftist cause in Spain. It was said in defense of a musi-

223

cian with a questionable wartime reputation that he couldn't convert anyone to Fascism by playing Bach. It may be said with equal assurance that a reading of *Four Saints* and *Tender Buttons* will not persuade anyone to vote a reactionary ticket.

$\mathcal{I}$T IS A NECESSITY
DESIRABLY TO UNITEDLY
ADMIRE ME

1

Appetite comes with eating, according to a French proverb, and Miss Stein's appetite for publication, recognition and financial reward grew with every little bite. "Think of the Bible and Homer think of Shakespeare and think of me," she wrote in *The Geographical History of America*, where she also claimed that "in this epoch the only real literary thinking has been done by a woman." Naturally it was embarrassing when editors stubbornly rejected that woman's works.

This egotism is ridiculed easily, yet in fairness to Miss Stein we must ask whether she wasn't driven to it in part because she had something to sell and needed the money. "Is money money?" she inquired, and more than once she complained to me that there weren't enough buyers for her product, and when there were they paid but little. No one depreciates his own bill of goods, especially when he is down to his last cent as Miss Stein and Miss Toklas were at several periods.

At the opening of her career, when she could afford to live comfortably in Paris, buy paintings, meet and entertain the most interesting people and write at leisure, she could anticipate with some confidence an intriguing and satisfying future rich in achievements. Though she later called those the tormented years, they brought with them many compensations. When *Three Lives* was published, she delightedly hired a clipping service; when *Lucy Church Amiably* inaugurated the Plain Editions undertaken by Miss Toklas, she tramped the streets proudly in search of copies in bookstore windows. There was no final, conclusive failure. There was always hope.

Yet as decade after decade passed, as she reached forty, fifty and sixty, she was obliged to wonder why, in a world full of publishers all busy publishing books, more of her works were not printed. A friend trying to borrow rare Steiniana from some acquaintances learned of missing items and comforted Miss Stein by saying that, if she wasn't the best-selling author, she was the best stolen. But that did not alter or soften the harsh fact that the old shoulder-high chest in which she stored typed manuscripts was filled nearly to the top.

It was all the more irritating because many of her followers, so classified by them or by critics, were minting money. Once when I commented heedlessly on fresh successes by Ernest Hemingway and Louis Bromfield, I realized that I had touched a tender spot:

"The Hem Louis made me sad because they earn so

much money, when I think Paris France brought me less than a thousand and the Winner Loses $250 and yet it was read all over the world and Ida which seems much loved only $350, it is sad . . . it would be nice to make money, so nice, well anyway . . . ."

She had confessed in *Everybody's* that while she wanted to get rich, she had never wanted "to do what there is to do to get rich," and though it did hurt, she could laugh about it. She was laughing, too, though perhaps sourly, when she wrote that she was at last starting a popular novel, and added: "Popular with whom?" And there is a wistful sentence in *The Making of Americans:* "Bear it in mind my reader, but truly I never feel it that there ever can be for me any such creature." At my hint that the new wartime experiences would make a grand book which I would love and by which I would be moved, she replied:

"Yes perhaps I will write how it all is, I like to make you cry and to make money, bless you both."

As would have happened without my suggestion, both books and articles developed out of the trying days following 1939: "I am beginning to write while the memory is still vivid just what we did during that time. I have already begun it just a short thing I call Sundays and Tuesdays do you think some magazine would like to pay me a thousand dollars or so for it, we could use money now . . . ."

In December, 1941, her account of this continued, still with the emphasis on money: "Just had a letter from the Atlantic that is from Edward Weeks and they seem also moved to tears by my mss, but not alas moved to very much money, they pay $250 which is alright but might be more I am writing to him to that effect, you could not live long in the U.S. on that, but here it helps quite a lot." ["Sundays and Tuesdays" was printed under another and, I thought, less apposite title, "The Winner Loses."]

Sales, and sizes of editions, were of primary concern, and she referred to them frequently as in these sentences culled from the letters of several years:

"The Atlantic took one and is meditating the second one . . . Jay Laughlin has just printed another one in New Directions, May d'Aiguy is translating them . . . I had a charming letter from [Ellery] Sedgwick and they [the *Atlantic*] have taken them both and sent me a check and I am as happy as happy can be about it . . . The Picasso book is almost ready to print . . . The English edition of Everybody's is to be out March 7 . . . The first edition of Picasso is about sold out 7500 not so bad in 3 months [1938] . . . The contract for the English edition of the Picasso is signed with Batsford in London and he did not succeed in arranging for the American edition with Cerf [of Random House] and Scribners are to do it . . . A publishing house William R. Scott, New York have asked me to write them a children's story and I am rather taken with the idea . . . I have sold the World is Round to Harpers Bazar . . . My editor tells me that they have tried out the World is Round on groups of children and there is no doubt of its effectiveness, so we will hope that all babies will cry for it, and we will get rich and live long and prosper all of us . . . The Paris, France is being printed, Batsfords seem very xcited, it is to have 8 illustrations . . . They sold into the third thousand of the World is Round by the end of December, not so bad, does it go on selling after Christmas, I hope so . . . I have just had a letter from Bennett Cerf, they xpect to do Ida just after New Year."

Miss Toklas recalls that while her friend had a sense for business affairs in the large, she was less attentive to little things. Only one item in a publisher's contract mattered to her, after the stipulation about payment, and it required an unfortunate experience to teach her to check on that: she always demanded a release clause calling for the return of a manuscript still unprinted after eighteen months. Nevertheless she at least knew that bread was supposed to be buttered on one side or the other. In one letter she asked about a publisher:

"I would like to know if it is an all right publisher, is he honest and is he possible, please let me know as soon as possible because I might have to agree soon."

On another occasion she wrote: "My child's story [*The World Is Round*] is about done, it is good, the Scott people made me one of those gentlemen's printers propositions, and I declined it politely whereupon they sent me a long cable saying they did not mean what they said but wanted it dreadfully, now I have made them a counter proposition, and that is where we are now."

This episode, like the book itself, ended happily: "And a funny thing has happened, the editors practically said no and then to my great astonishment day before yesterday the post office said they had lots of money for me, ah said I, yes they said did you not know, no, I said, well anyway there it was a nice advance and presumably from Scott, I thought it might be Scribners, I never thought it was Scott although it was the right sum for Scott and not for Scribners and then a cable saying yes letter follows."

One publisher's "solemn contract with rising scale of royalties" was in her opinion "an encouraging thing to see in intention."

During the discussion of a second lecture tour in America, Van Vechten suggested it would be wise to get all the money deposited to her credit in a bank before she left France. She thought it "would be nice if that being once done, one might go over and enjoy oneself and not lecture . . . It is pleasant toying with the idea of prospective wealth." Concerning a writer who wired for permission to quote her in a book of criticism, and prepaid the reply, she asked me: "So is he rich or only just foolish?"

In one exuberant postwar letter she said: "The last climax was the Play, Yes is for a very young man has finally had its option sold to some young people one of them Johnston [Lamont Johnson] may come and see you and tell you all about it and us, and there is a lot to tell, if they do give it in Pasadena [they did] well Alice says we got to go [they didn't], Brewsie and Willie the G-I book Random House will be out just about then too, some time in March, and I guess all that would be too xciting, Paris is occupying but not xciting, however, we'll see. I've never seen anything like it, I said to Alice, we can't sell any more books because we have no more to sell, sold 4 to Italy the other day, editions in Sweden, Geneva, and now [a New York firm] wants to do my other child book To Do, the one First Reader is sold to England, to think how hard it used to be to get anybody to do anything, anyway it's nice to be glorious and popular in your old age, and to buy bones for Basket and be admired by the young, well bless you kiddies bless you . . ."

2

Miss Stein was, perhaps after Miss Toklas, her own dearest friend and friendliest critic. If some readers have been offended by the conceit revealed in her books, they will possibly be more lenient when they realize that it is not so much vanity as naïvete. Formally she wrote "for myself and strangers," she declared, and so it didn't matter whether she sounded too forward. But in her correspondence with me the tone is no longer insistent; she involves me in it with her, I share her conceit and so, oddly, it ceases to be conceit; it's a confidence, it's a fond assumption, we take on together a sort of proud-parent attitude, and rather than disapprove of it, I like it, as it occurs in these stray sentences from nearly a score of letters:

"I have just done a play which is pretty good and I have just started another which is better. I kind of think it is my best . . . I am pleased with the first assistant [in 1937, Joseph Barber, Jr., managing editor] of the Atlantic monthly, I have just sent them to tease them 2 short stories of Bilignin I have just written which I think are rather nice . . . May d'Aiguy is translating them all and they do go well in french . . . A funny little portrait I did to please the D'Aiguys I think it rather sweet . . . The ballet [in London] a great success, everybody very xcited and we had to come out and bow, it was very wonderful, and we liked it all . . . The Atlantic was I think ["Butter Will Melt," 1937] xtraordinarily well done, it gave me a lot of pleasure to read it . . . We are awfully pleased with everything . . . [*The World Is Round*] is nice . . . [The Batsford book] is very well done . . . I have done an article for the London Harpers about English painting in Paris which everybody seems to like [the article, of course, not the painting] . . . I have once more begun the great American novel [1939] . . . I guess it is going to be a pretty book . . . [*Ida*] is going nicely . . . I am greatly pleased with [*Mrs. Reynolds*] . . . I think in a kind of way [*Brewsie and Willie*] is one of the best things I have ever done."

These wishful feelers that she throws out remind us sadly that in order to be sure of any indorsement of some of her works, she must indorse them herself. But they are interspersed with direct appeals to me to approve of what she has written, and in the quotations below I find some of the most touching words in all her letters:

"You will like it."

"I think you will like it."

"Will you send it to Thornton [Wilder] and will you both like it and tell us so."

"I think it is pretty handsome and hope you will think so too."

"By this time you will have read it and liked it I hope."

232

"You will be having Paris France by now and I hope liking it."

"I hope you like it."

"Write me all about it."

"How pleased we were that you were."

Her friends expected her to be frank, about herself as well as about them, and would have been disappointed if she had failed them. Carl Van Vechten once wrote me about a quotation from her book *To Do* that he "knew I would love":

> "Nobody is so rude
> Not to remember Gertrude."

Whenever the opportunity offered, she naturally varied her self-praise with praise from others, as on the occasion of the French edition of the *Picasso:*

"Madame Clermont-Tonnerre says it is magnificent genial, does not need any changing, is claire [clear] and nette [plain], make anybody understand not only Picasso but 19 and 20 centuries and the universe, and painting and writing, well anything you like."

From the way she wound that up, she may have feared the praise was a trifle exaggerated, or may have imagined I'd think so. Yet at the very next chance, she was writing, and again with that quick note of apology at the end to redeem it all: "Everybody is quite mad about" the child's story, and "Alice thinks it's the best I have ever done, well anyway . . ." Henry Kahnweiler of the Galeries Simon came to her rescue about *Paris France:* "It is a most resembling portrait of France, so loving and so moving, so direct, so true, so you see," Miss Stein added, "how pleased I am."

She could blow her own horn, gay or melancholy, better probably than anyone else. Hostile criticism from the press was no particular pleasure to her but she learned to endure it, though she claimed that the person who needs criticism is not an artist at all . . . Osbert Sitwell, who "abhors and abominates" criticism, isn't the only one to agree with her. What she resented was not the rebuff by the critic but the rejection by the publishing house. Of a children's story which she was unable to place she wrote me:

"It is a kind of book I would have liked as a child, more than I would have liked the World is Round." She amplified that: "I am so sure that when I was a child I would have liked it that I do not understand, and I see a good many children these days and they like the stories, I do remain puzzled, but being puzzled is natural to me so I must not complain."

Contrasted with this bewilderment was her jubilation on receiving copies of *Everybody's Autobiography*:

"I am so xcited about the book I can't tell you . . . I must say that I read it through from cover to cover and I was fascinated, I thing it is an xtraordinarily fascinating book and really everybody's autobiography, anyway that is the way I feel about it."

Here again she abandoned all restraint and then recovered herself with the little embarrassed concluding phrase. In her books it was different; there she put her best foot forward and stamped it down to stay. "I am a rare one," she cried in *The Making of Americans*, with no apology to soften it. When Gertrude Stein really concentrated on praising Gertrude Stein, she was expert at it, as in "Three Sitting Here" from *Portraits and Prayers:*

"Everyone singly and together admired me. They have seen it because which is why when and surrounded by amending what has been added and reasoning reasoning is there and left alone with their very carefully withdrawn complimenting in assistance. It is by this time that they are and mine. There is every reason for the greeting with which they do not deny that they do not need to try to believe that it is a necessity desirably to unitedly admire me. In reality to excitedly admire me. They do admire me. In their admiring of me there is connectedly a reunion of their celebrating their admiration for me and of me."

In thanking me for a newsphoto included in a batch of clippings of the *Champlain* press conference, at which I sat grinning happily behind her while she parried questions, she wrote:

"I like the way you look so proud of me, I do like that."

Since that was exactly the way I felt, I am sure it must have been the way I looked.

3

Miss Stein wrote a great deal about how to write. While she did not regard herself as an experimentalist, a word which implies the amateur, she was a theorist, filled with ideas about composition, description, narration and so

235

on, and she devoted lectures, essays and books to these subjects.

She talked about them, too, yet did not put much about them in her letters. While she told me a lot about what she got out of her prose, she told little about what she got into it. That may have been due partly to the personal nature of our correspondence which, as I look back over it, has few references to the craft of writing and fewer still to her contemporaries practising it.

"I never could read Bromfield [her very good friend, nevertheless], not any, and hardly any of Glenway [Wescott]," she wrote me in 1945 when I offered to send her Wescott's *Apartment in Athens*, which I liked. We reminded Miss Stein of her comment in the Toklas *Autobiography* to the effect that this author had a syrup that did not pour. She answered:

"Now his syrup pours but it is stickier than ever," and continued: "The comparison does seem a bit useless now doesn't it, and do you think I really said it, I do not really think I did no really not, however if he thinks so it is alright, is he still socially xclusive, he announced one winter that he was going to be to all our delight . . ."

Antagonisms of this nature, and they were not rare, were customarily mutual. It was of course those with whom she shared warm feelings of affection who were most influenced by either her writing or her personality. But her guidance was not academic; it did not often include such specific recommendations as the admonishment to Ernest Hemingway: remarks do not make literature. When she advised him to abandon newspaper work

236

and gamble his savings on a year of creative writing, he followed her advice, settled in the Hôtel Trianon in Paris and produced *The Sun Also Rises*. He has not at any time denied openly his indebtedness to her, and he has refrained from any of the retorts she might have been expected to incite. She was always fond of him, and when she made fun of him in the bull-fight game with Basket at Bilignin, she acted with wit and without malice.

She would often disclose what a book was going to be like: *Everybody's Autobiography* was to be "mostly about the simple life and the early Stein family . . . written very simply, perhaps too simply." Inspired by the books displayed in the stalls by the Seine, *Mrs. Reynolds*, "an old fashioned novel," threatened to become "a dictator novel." And there was always the light touch. While she was busy on her *Faust*, of which "I think there will be 4 acts," Jay Laughlin said that "in America they would make it Gertie's Faust." Laboring on *Yes Is for a Very Young Man*, she reported "two scenes done then I get stuck but I guess I will get unstuck." Of *The Mother of Us All* she admitted that "how much it is an opera this I do not know" but declared "it goes well and I like it."

She was more informative about the first war book:

"Alas the U.S. Army is dwindling and dwindling and what there is left has not really the authentic G.I. flavor, but I do think that I did get into Brewsie and Willie the book that Bennett [Cerf] is doing this spring, I did get that authentic flavor . . . You know how much I have always meditated about Narration, how to tell what one has to tell, well this time I have gotten it, narration as the 20 century sees it, the English think I have done something new in it."

If she resembled most authors in being an unreliable judge of her own works, she resembled all authors in the unevenness of her production. Some books are worth more than the others. Some of them should have been edited, or even cut remorselessly. She appreciated that herself, I think, for she acknowledged that the four-hundred-page French edition of *The Making of Americans* did not suffer severely by comparison with the original thousand-page English version.

In directing the posthumous publication of her remaining manuscripts, she acted on the conviction that, since the passage of time had disclosed the indubitable importance of her early work, so would her late work, if given a chance, win eventual recognition. For some writers, like Flaubert, as for some painters, like Cézanne or Ryder, a work is never finished; to the day of their death they could keep on improving it. For others, like Miss Stein, a work is finished as soon as it is inscribed.

It is no real service to her—and I should like always to be of service to her and to her memory—to invite the public to pick up any volume indiscriminately, for they are not of equal worth. In addition to her very special contributions to literature, there are spread through all her writing, for the delectation of the diligent new reader, a diversity of rhythms, many profound and searching observations, much wit, and extremely quotable remarks, of exactly the kind for which she chided Ernest Hemingway. But some books abound in discouraging pages, and other volumes, it seems to me, are more notebook than finished work, even though to her they were complete; they are the inception, not the development, of ideas, more interesting after you know Gertrude Stein than when you are trying to make her acquaintance. For making her acquaintance, nothing is better than *The Autobiography of Alice B. Toklas.* As for the less traditional works, *Three Lives* should properly come first. *The Making of Americans* deserves try after try, and preferably in the abridged American edition; taken slowly, and not too much at a time, it will prove rewarding. After that, *Tender Buttons* is essential, for here is the kind of Stein that launched a thousand jibes; this represents the big break with the sort of books to which we had been accustomed, and once you have succumbed to it, you can take anything, you have become a Stein reader. *Lucy Church Amiably, Operas and Plays, Four Saints* and *Four in America* are to be recommended. But *Brewsie and Willie, Wars I Have Seen* and *Yes Is for a Very Young Man,* among the better known works, are less stimulating despite some excellent passages. Some of the later writing has gone slack, it is diffused, and we hunt in vain for the verve of the *Autobiography* and the evocative power of *Four Saints* and the incomparable charm of "Rose is a rose is a rose is a rose."

"Rose is a rose" is a simple, unarguable statement of fact, a phrase for a copybook, an elementary declarative sentence beginning with a capital and ending with a period.

"Rose is a rose is a rose is a rose" has been laughed off as a tipsy way of turning one rose into Four Roses.

But to some people, myself among them, it represents one method by which a writer has bridged successfully the immeasurable distance from grammar to literature. In Miss Stein's famous version we have a kind of chant, rhythmic, gentle and soothing, an extension of enjoyment. Primarily sensuous, these words evoke, if we let them alone to work their magic, the color, odor and grace of the flower.

In this instance, as in others, the poetry of Miss Stein is Miss Stein. She had a habit in which she indulged most often while she drove; with her left elbow on the ledge of the opened car window, her thumb and forefinger pinched repeatedly at a strand of hair above her ear. This pull and tug and twist and roll of the hair in her fingers is another extension of enjoyment, a caress. Just as she feels the cropped tuft, so she feels a word. The subtly erotic gesture becomes the subtly erotic phrase, and the sensation in her fingertips, by an act of absolutely pure creative writing, flows off the fingertips to the paper, so to speak, and is imparted to the reader. A caress is a caress is a caress is a caress is a "rose is a rose is a rose is a rose."

It was Miss Toklas who rescued the memorable line from oblivion. Finding it among some scattered papers, she recognized it as the essence of Stein the writer and Stein the person . . . the Gertrude Stein who, even more than Henry James, whose words these are, wanted "to live in the world of creation—to get in it and stay in it—to frequent it and haunt it."

$\mathcal{N}$OT A SADNESS

THE AMERICAN SEVENTH ARMY, speeding north from the Mediterranean, liberated Culoz in August, 1944, and with it Miss Stein and Miss Toklas.

Miss Stein met soldiers, officers and newsmen with wide-open arms, hugs and kisses, and led them off to Miss Toklas' breakfast, dinner or supper at the château. This was the day they had prayed for, thus was fulfilled the prophecy of Johannes the monk and St. Odile and St. Kiddie, here was the hour of deliverance heralded by the rattle of jeeps, the tramp of shoes with real leather soles, and the welcomed and beloved voices of New York, Chicago, San Francisco and Boston.

Miss Stein spent her time being vociferously jubilant; Miss Toklas divided hers between pots and pans and the typewriter on which she rushed to completion the manuscript of *Wars I Have Seen* so that Frank Gervasi of *Collier's*, who was to fly back to the States immediately, could bring a copy for the publisher and also, to Miss Stein's American friends, the first letters they had received in two years.

Then the two city-bred women, feeling as if they

never wanted to set foot in the country again, returned to rue Christine. In the dilapidated car in which they traveled, with Miss Toklas packed in solid among household goods and the Picasso portrait, it was an exhausting day-and-night journey, broken alarmingly in a pitch-dark wood by an armed Resistance band which demanded and received an accounting.

Except for the hasty visit to rescue a couple of paintings, this was the first time they had seen Paris since the spring of 1939. The apartment had been vacant during the occupation, but the invaders had not overlooked it. They stole every stitch of linen and every piece of silver stored in drawers and cupboards, and almost made away with the pictures, too. They removed a fortune in art from the walls, stacked it on the floors and tied it up ready to cart off, but a vigilant gendarme caught them at it and managed to effect enough of a delay so that the Germans had to abandon their loot and run to save their skins when the capital was liberated.

For her two remaining years Miss Stein was free to savor all the sweet there can be in literary and personal renown. Few writers live to enjoy such a phenomenal apotheosis. Some of the GI's had heard her lecture in the States; some knew her books; but even the ignorant, passing her striking figure in the street, could tell she was "a rare one." Wherever she went, the soldiers recognized her:

"Hello, Miss Stein . . . You're Gertrude Stein . . . Aren't you Miss Stein . . . Hi, Gert!"

At every salutation she stopped, yes I am Miss Stein, yes this is Gert. The Yanks accosted her alone, Miss

Toklas alone, and both of them together. Many knew her address and went directly to the rue Christine, asked the bent, withered and unshaven old concierge where her apartment was, raced up the wide stairs, pushed the bell, aroused Basket to furious barking, and were admitted.

She had been starved for Americans, and was overjoyed at this flood of uniformed callers. "You can only visit your native land after thirty-one years once," she had remarked ruefully following the 1934–35 trip, and she hadn't crossed the ocean since then. Now her native land had come to her. If New York had been a Christmas tree, this was a three-ring circus. She entertained the men by day and in the evening, at lunch and tea, with long discussions but with no strong drink, for she never found tipsters amusing and expected visitors to be stimulating, as she was, without stimulants. She argued with them under her own roof and under theirs when she was a guest at army mess and when she and Miss Toklas went on a five-day air tour of United States posts in occupied Germany, where the writer and the soldiers indulged in heart-to-heart talks . . . "You will see all about it in Life," she wrote us.

Some of them paid only one call, others still visit Miss Toklas, among them the "Jo the Loiterer" of *The Mother of Us All*, a State department official, some authors, artists and students. One of them told me as we left Miss Toklas' one evening that he had been wandering along the rue de Rivoli when he caught a glimpse of the women at tea in Rumpelmayer's, stopped and stared, and was invited in by Miss Toklas. His experience probably was duplicated again and again.

During her American tour Miss Stein as a person created an impression the full extent of which it would be difficult to exaggerate. The interest shown in her was flattering, but she would gladly have shared it with her writing. Yet the truth is, the writing appeared to be subject to argument, and the person wasn't and isn't. Bernard Faÿ expressed it perfectly: "The greatest and most beautiful of her gifts is her presence." A young Wisconsin student sent to interview her for the University paper was expected to bring back one of the supposedly funny stories about Stein Stein in Madison Madison, and was so swept off his feet that twelve years later the awe still sounded in his voice when he spoke of her. A young New Yorker, now a publisher, brought away from the Brooklyn lecture such an overpowering admiration for her that he began to proselyte in her name, gained one fair listener and talked Stein to her until she married him.

Over many people Miss Stein cast a sort of spell, and what had happened in America in the strictly formal atmosphere surrounding the visiting celebrity must have happened many more times in Paris. To the one Kiddie of World War I were now added a hundred and a thousand more. It wasn't a following she had, but a court. One young man introduced a friend, who introduced a friend, who introduced a friend. It was a chain process. It was the old days at the rue de Fleurus over again, when Ernest Hemingway was introduced to Miss Stein by Sherwood Anderson, and Anderson was introduced by Sylvia Beach, Carl Van Vechten by Mabel Dodge [Luhan], Virgil Thomson by George Antheil, and so on.

She has recorded the conversations of the new generation, the lively exchange as well as the dull, in *Brewsie and Willie*, for if Stein the person didn't change, neither did Stein the writer, and up to her last years she found her material under her nose. She made hay while she had fun.

But the fun waned, and months after Germany's defeat, when the soldiers in Paris became largely the recruits untried in battle, her interest slackened. The sessions began to tire her. She was, she wrote me, in need of a rest; in one letter she mentioned casually, as if it was no more important than the weather, a touch of digestive disorder. She bought a car and with Miss Toklas started for the country, again and for the last time to "forget the war a little." On a street corner near her apartment and Picasso's studio, she and the artist exchanged what proved to be their final farewells.

Before she and Miss Toklas had reached their destination, a home lent them for the summer months, she was stricken seriously and had to be rushed back to Paris. After keeping her under observation for a few days, doctors in the American hospital at Neuilly announced that they would not operate; the knife would probably kill her but could not possibly cure her.

"So many things begin around fifteen. Money, possessions, eternity, enemies, the fear of death," she had noted in one of her last books. Little of that fear remained by now, however. She was tired, and she was philosophical. At seventy-two she had come to realize, as she stated in *Wars I Have Seen*, that "you have to learn to do everything, even to die." She had had to learn, also, to endure the death of friends, and since she could experience great affection as well as inspire it, that lesson had been hard for her.

During the American tour she had renewed her close acquaintance with F. Scott Fitzgerald briefly in Baltimore where "he and I had a curious and very poignant time together," and after his death she wrote me: "Poor Fitzgerald I would have liked to have done something for him in memoriam, the three out of that old time together whom I really care for were Sherwood Hemingway and Fitzgerald." When Anderson, too, died as he was setting out for South America, a letter of Miss Stein's said: "I read with sadness the description of Sherwood's last illness. I wish he might have had his South American trip, he was so looking forward to it, he had written me about it just before he started, dear Sherwood." And in her only heavy-hearted letter to me during the war, in January, 1941, she said:

"Here we are in the New Year but it is a sad New Year because Mme Pierlot died night before last, she was accustomed to a warm house and it was cold and she loved to go up into the attic and rummage around and they could not stop her from doing it now and she took cold and it turned into pneumonia and she died and we are all so unhappy, she was very wonderful and we all will miss her dreadfully" . . . Those words might have served Miss Stein for an epitaph: "She was very wonderful and we all will miss her dreadfully."

Except for the immortality which her writing might bestow on her, Miss Stein had long since come to believe that "dead is dead," and she had the consolation of knowing that Miss Toklas shared this conception. She was not resigned to leaving the life she had so warmly loved and savored, and taught others to savor with her, but she was not afraid, and no less bravely than the American soldiers she had known in two wars, she insisted on an operation which she knew she could not survive. She had chosen her kind of life, said a friend, and so she chose her kind of death.

Failing to recover consciousness after the anaesthetic was administered, she died the afternoon of Saturday, July 27, 1946.

She was buried in Père-Lachaise cemetery beside a shaded and cobbled road. Her grave is marked by a border and headstone designed by her friend, the English painter Sir Francis Rose. One surface bears in square letters her name and the cities and dates of her birth and death; on the other side there will be sometime the name, and the cities and dates of birth and death, of Miss Toklas.

I am sure Miss Stein chose to stay among the French in death because the French way of life was infinitely precious to her. But during her life the French way of death had moved her deeply, too, and in the last days she must have remembered admiring how sagely her adopted people "feel about the dead, it is so friendly so simply friendly and though inevitable not a sadness and though occurring not a shock."